D0776865

A Mirror for Americanists

William C. Spengemann

A Mirror for Americanists

Reflections on the Idea of
American Literature

Published for Dartmouth College by
University Press of New England
Hanover and London

University Press of New England

Brandeis University	*Dartmouth College*
Brown University	*University of New Hampshire*
Clark University	*University of Rhode Island*
University of Connecticut	*Tufts University*
University of Vermont	

LIBRARY OF CONGRESS CATALOGING-IN-PUBLICATON DATA
Spengemann, William C.
  A mirror for Americanists.
  1. American literature—History and criticism—Theory, etc. I. Title.
PS25.S64 1989   810'.9   88-40354
ISBN 0-87451-478-9
ISBN 0-87451-483-5 (pbk.)

5 4 3 2 1

For Ori and, memorially, for Doc

Acknowledgments

The materials asssembled here have passed, in one form or another, through a good many capable hands and heads, acquiring encouragement and useful advice at every turn and increasing my debts far beyond hope of repayment. Listed in the approximate order of their impressment into the service of my errant vessel, the following people have been especially helpful and generous: Kenneth Lynn, Russell Nye, John Seelye, David Mead, Norman Grabo, Marco Portales, Milton Stern, Ralph Cohen, Robert Dawidoff, Ellen Graham, Peter Shaw, Sacvan Bercovitch, Everett Emerson, Nina Baym, Richard Ruland, James Cox, Donald Pease, Louis Renza, Blake Nevius, Thomas Wortham, Edwin Cady, Louis Budd, Robert Milder, Joseph Blotner, Leo Lemay, Peter Carafiol, Norman Council, William Cain, Philip Gura, David Laurence, Robert Weisbuch, and Charles Backus. Since my habit is always to hug encouragement and shun advice, none of these scholars can be blamed for anything that appears in the following pages. For permission to reprint materials published earlier, I am grateful to the editors of *Centennial Review, New Literary History, Early American Literature, Nineteenth-Century Literature, ELH,* and *American Literature,* and to Penguin-Viking, Inc., publishers of my edition of Henry James's *The American.*

Contents

Introduction

The essays in this volume record my reflections, over the past several years, on the idea of American literature: the general understanding of this subject, held by virtually all practicing Americanists, that tells us which texts to teach and study and what to say about them. These reflections began back in 1977 when, struggling to produce some jacket copy for an impending book on nineteenth-century American fiction, I found myself pondering the assumption that had enabled me to write the book: the notion that American fiction is a distinct entity whose character can be described, its origins discovered, and its development traced.

Where had I got the idea that certain novels written in English at various times in the nineteenth century by assorted Americans constitute something called The American Novel, different from The English Novel and possessed of a history of its own? The idea seemed to be generally accepted. I had never heard its logic seriously questioned, and (as some reviewers of the book would feel obliged to point out) my conception of the subject was hardly a new departure. On the contrary, the book has arisen out of a course in American fiction much like those taught in classrooms all over the country, and it ended up on a shelf in the library already well supplied with studies of the same subject.

Nevertheless, the more I turned this idea over in my mind, the less reasonable it seemed. If The American Novel means anything, I supposed, it must mean the novel as Americans have written it— a category far too large and various to allow much in the way of striking generalization, especially by someone like myself, who had not read very many American novels beyond the handful treated in my book. Those I had discussed were, for the most part, the ones usually found in courses and studies in The American

Novel—*The Scarlet Letter, Moby-Dick, Huckleberry Finn,* and the rest. Had some energetic group of Americanists once read all of the novels ever written in this country and decided that these were the most representative, the most American? If not, they could not very well provide a basis for statements about The American Novel—unless, of course, they constituted The American Novel all by themselves, in which case The American Novel must mean the novels that Americanists talk about when they talk about The American Novel.

Less than reassured by these reflections, I turned to American poetry, the second most common topic of college courses and learned monographs in the field. Was it not an equally mysterious category, one cobbled together on some obscure principle from parts of three more coherent categories: poems in English, poems by Americans, and good poems? Why should poems in English by Americans be separated, on the one hand, from poetry in English by Canadians and, on the other, from poems by Americans in Spanish or Chinese? If poems in English by Americans are American, authorial nationality, not language, is definitive, and poetry written by Americans in other languages must be American as well. Why, in addition, does the study of American poetry give preference to poems of high literary quality? Are these more American, more representative of what American poets have written, than mediocre ones? In any case, how can a body of poetry so constituted possibly have the identity and continuity that Americanists regularly claim for American poetry?

My inability to answer these seemingly basic questions led directly to the suspicion that American literature itself—the field in which I had been trained, in which I had been teaching and writing for a good many years, and in which I had come to fancy myself an expert—might be an altogether imaginary subject; not a self-evident set of books lying out there in the world, waiting to be studied, but merely an idea, with very little in the way of solid evidence to support it.

At the same time, I could not help suspecting that I had overlooked something obvious, some crucial step in the logic by which the idea of American literature had been arrived at, some definitive sign by which Americanists recognize a piece of American literature when they see one. As I say, no other Americanists seemed to share my skepticism, and it struck me as unlikely that the entire institution of American literature, with all of its professorships, publications, courses, degrees, and the like, could rest upon an illusion sufficiently evident for me to detect and yet invisible to everyone else. Unless the institution was engaged in a vast conspiracy to foist a counterfeit subject upon an unsuspecting world, then either Americanists were wrapped in their own dogmatic slumbers, or I had simply missed the point.

To test the ground beneath my growing doubts, I wrote "What Is American Literature?—the essay that opens this volume—casting my uncertainties regarding the subject in the form of an attack on its sponsoring institution. Surely, I supposed, my readers would either point out the holes in my argument—in which case I could return, chastened, to business—or else join me in the task of reconstructing the foundations on which our collective enterprise rests.

In the event, neither of these things happened. When, after having been rejected by *American Literature* as unsuited to the aims of that journal, the essay appeared in *Centennial Review,* one or two people wrote to express their concurrence in its findings. Otherwise, my little device exploded without attracting much attention. No one felt called upon to defend the notions and practices I had attacked or to show where my reasoning had left the road. But neither could I take this silence as a plea of nolo contendere, since American literature went on peddling its usual wares at the same old stand as if no charges had been brought against it. Not even *American Literary Scholarship* found the essay worth mentioning in its annual survey of work in the field, despite my having taken the precaution of sending the editors an offprint.

Now I was really puzzled. Did Americanists simply not read the piece even when it was thrust upon them? Surely, they could not have read it without feeling obliged either to rebut my charges or to alter their own way of doing things. Was the argument perhaps too obscure to permit some sort of response or too ridiculous to deserve one? Or did the profession just have its own music turned up so loud that I could not be heard rummaging around in the cellar? One thing at least was clear: those who did read the essay did not regard it as a message intended for them. To whom had I been speaking? Who entertained the baseless ideas I was questioning? Who were the perpetrators of this delusion called American literature, and who were its victims?

Returning to the essay with these questions in mind, I was struck first of all by its steeply condescending attitude and then by the perfect familiarity of the person upon whom it looked down so contemptuously. True to its reflective origins, my polemic retained, clearly imprinted upon its rhetorical surface, the image of my own long-held and only recently abandoned assumptions. Whether or not anyone else was listening, I was certainly talking to myself—or rather to that mindlessly credulous person who had been teaching my classes and writing my books all those years. No wonder my colleagues had failed to hear my indictment. Even someone who happened to harbor the views assaulted there might understandably decline to own them in that unattractive guise.

If I expected to "open an intercourse with the world," it was clear that I would have to cultivate a more ingratiating style of address. Most Americanists, I knew, can take a point perfectly well without having to be scolded; and since I was in fact criticizing my own ideas, a reflective attitude would more accurately portray the true character of my statements, as well as place the reader safely behind the cannon. Sound policy, however, would prove no match for temperament and habit. As the essays that make up the remainder of this volume plainly show, my efforts to maintain a posture of cool consideration have been largely unsuccessful. Whenever reflection discovers among my memories of former lectures and publications an especially fatuous, altogether unsupportable notion, impatience unseats inquiring reason and begins to hector.

No doubt the purpose of these essays would be better served were they revised to address their intended audience directly, rather than by way of a straw man fashioned from my own discarded ideas. Experience has repeatedly proved their manner both counterproductive and unnecessary. On the other hand, they owe whatever force they have to exasperation, and to disown that enabling spirit would be no less ungrateful than is their condemnation of the follies that permit them to feel wise. Although their tone occasionally impedes persuasion, the reader can overcome that obstacle simply by remembering that they really are reflections. Taken in that spirit, they may provide an aid, and perhaps a spur, to reflections of the reader's own.

Were I to write these pieces today, they would look very different. Not only have they taught me things I hardly suspected when I began, but more important, the profession of American literature has undergone significant changes over the same period. In 1978, American literary scholarship seemed to be adrift in the horse latitudes, having been blown there by the winds of the American Studies movement and the New Criticism and then suddenly becalmed. Since then, the demographic character of the profession has changed, and both the canon and the methods of studying it have changed apace to reflect the interests of this new constituency. Not since the 1950s perhaps have American literary studies been so lively, wide-ranging, and self-aware.

In another, and to my mind more fundamental, respect, however, nothing has changed. While ideas about American literature have shifted dramatically, the idea of American literature remains essentially the one I labored to define in 1978. As our most recent histories of the subject indicate, the American literature that is taught and studied throughout the profession still consists almost entirely of writings in English by Americans that will lend themselves to literary use. As a result, "American" still does not define a sort of literature, "literature" still does not define a particular sort of writing, and "American literature" still implies something far more specific and distinct than the facts of the matter will support.

Until we can explain how a piece of writing, in whatever language, is itself American and not just written by one, American literature won't be American. Until we can distinguish between literature and other sorts of writing, it won't be literature. And until we can show a direct logical relation between what makes a piece of writing American and what makes it literature, it won't be American literature. In the meantime, the questions raised in these essays will retain their cogency, and my reflections their utility as a mirror in which Americanists may perhaps catch a glimpse of themselves.

What Is American Literature?

Everyone knows what American literature is. When we tell people that we are students or teachers or critics or scholars of American literature, they don't ask what that means. And it is lucky for us that they do not ask, for we might find it embarrassingly difficult to come up with a definition of the subject we actually study, teach, and write about. We cannot say, for example, that American literature is literature written in America. In the first place, that explanation explains nothing. It simply raises two additional and even more difficult questions: "What is literature?" and "What is America?" And in the second place, this definition does not square with the kind of statement we like to make about the subject.

If someone says that American literature is idealistic, he does not mean that all literature written in America is idealistic. He means that the idealism of certain works written in America is what makes them American. Furthermore, when someone else says that American literature is realistic, he does not necessarily mean that those works written in America which have sometimes been considered as idealistic are actually realistic, or even that they are idealistic as well as realistic. For he may be talking about altogether different works—realistic ones rather than idealistic ones.

The clear implication of such statements is that although all American literature is written in America, not all literature written in America is American literature. American literature, therefore, must be the works we make statements about—the ones we teach in our courses, include in our bibliographies and anthologies, and write about in our articles and monographs. American literature, in short, is what we do, and the definition of our subject must be found not in what American writers have done but in the multifarious actions we ourselves perform in the name of American literature. If we can formulate the definition that is implied by our activities, perhaps we can decide how well this definition serves our avowed aims and whether some other definition might not give us more help in our search for that elusive quality we call literary Americanness.

I

We can arrive at the definition that informs our current practice by starting with what the phrase "American literature" appears to denote on the face of it and then gradually modifying that definition in the light of what we actually do. At first glance, "American literature" seems to denote something both comprehensive and specific, something akin to "French literature" or "Russian literature." The grammatical resemblance is misleading, however, for, unlike its apparent analogues, "American literature" does not mean literature written in the language designated by the adjective. Although a great deal of work has been done on the subject, we do not yet have an acceptable definition of the American language. What is more, even if we had such a definition, and even if the language it described were to prove something more than a variety of English, few if any of the works now understood to constitute American literature would turn out to have been written in it.

On the contrary, the American literature that all but a very few of us teach and study is written in English. Therefore, "American literature" seems to mean not "literature written in American" but *literature written in English in America*—not in its own language but in its own place. To say that, however, is to trade an easy problem for a hard one: What place? Although the word "America" can be used quite correctly to designate either North America or South America separately, or the New World as a whole, among the practitioners of American literature the word clearly does not refer to any of those places, for our studies always exclude the literatures of South and Central America and customarily omit those of Mexico and Canada.

Is the geography of American literature, then, political rather than physical? Is our "America" simply a short title for "the United States of America"? The name of the standard history and bibliography of the subject, *The Literary History of the United States*, would appear to support that inference. The materials covered by those volumes, on the other hand, raise two further problems. First, if "American literature" really did mean "literature written in English in the United States," its history could begin no earlier than the Declaration of Independence. But neither the contents of the *LHUS* nor anything in our current practice implies any serious disagreement with Howard Mumford Jones's unhedged assertion that "American literature is as old as Jamestown." Second, "literature written in English in the United States" would have to omit the work of our expatriates, whereas the *LHUS*, like our courses and scholarship, includes such writers as Henry James, Gertrude Stein, and T. S. Eliot. It would appear, then, that in practice we project our political boundaries back to 1607 and extend U.S. literary citizenship to our writers abroad. If so, "American literature" as we practice it must mean *literature written in any place that is now part of the United States or by anyone who has ever lived in one of those places.*

So much for our operating definition of "American." But what about "literature"? Starting once again with what the word appears to mean on the face of it, we may note that *Webster's New World Dictionary of the American Language* conveniently provides a definition of "literature" in company with the modifier in question: "all the writings of a particular time, country, region, etc.: as, *American* literature." Even with the several qualifications we have placed upon the word "American," the body of material embraced by this definition is still much larger than the one to which we normally address ourselves. Although the contents of *The Cambridge History of American Literature* suggest that "literature" included virtually every form of literacy when the academic study of American literature began in earnest, fifty years ago, we need only review the succession of bibliographies that have guided our studies since then—*The Literary History of the United States, Eight American Authors,* and *American Literary Scholarship*—to see how the meaning of the word has gradually narrowed until "literature" now refers almost exclusively to poetry, fiction, and drama.

To be sure, important work has been done over the years in the so-called nonfictional genres: humor, biography, autobiography, travel writing, sermons, tracts, and the like. Nevertheless, only in a few striking instances have these putatively unliterary or subliterary materials been treated as literature rather than as sources of information about something else. Otherwise, the mainstream of American literary study continues to run well within the deep but narrow channel of belles lettres laid out by critics like Stedman and Brownell and subsequently cast in concrete by the New Criticism. As a result, most of the courses, books, and articles that now purport to deal with American literature might be more accurately described as treating nothing more than *poetry, fiction, and plays written in any place that is now part of the United States or by anyone who has ever lived in one of those places.*

Actually, our courses and scholarship concern themselves with far less writing than even this severely modified definition suggests. Our studies of the American novel provide a case in point. According to the operating definition of American literature we have arrived at so far, "American novel" would mean any novel written in English in any place that is now part of the United States or by anyone who has ever lived in one of those places. But that cannot be what the phrase means in practice, for we are forever making propositions about the subject. When we say that "American fiction is realistic" or that "the American novel is a romance," or anything of the sort, we are certainly not talking about *all* of the novels ever written in English by Americans. In the first place, we have not read them all. And in the second place, the contents of the category thus defined are far too various to permit any further predication whatsoever, let alone the kind of sweeping generalizations we like to make about "the American novel" and its national character.

When we offer such propositions, therefore, we must have in mind *some* American novels. The question is, which ones? Do we mean the most *important* ones? If so, what makes the novels we have selected "important" beyond the fact that they happen to support the particular proposition we have made concerning them? Is it that they are *representative*? Surely not, since we have not read all of the novels they supposedly represent and so cannot possibly know whether or not they are typical. Do we mean, then, the most *American* ones, as it sometimes appears? In that case, "American" clearly denotes something more specific than "written in English in any place that is now part of the United States or by anyone who has ever lived in one of those places," and we ought to say what. Or do such propositions refer only to the *best* American novels, our classics? If that is our principle of selection—as the works most often discussed in our courses and writings on the American novel strongly suggest—and if "best" is not merely a synonym for "most important" or "most American," then the novels covered by our propositions have been singled out for discussion because they measure up artistically to the great novels of the world and not because they are American.

By extending this final, aesthetic principle of selection from the American novel to American literature as a whole, we come at last to a definition of the subject we actually study, teach, and write about. Although "American literature" seems to designate a very large body of material, and although our habitual parlance implies that the works we call American are uniquely or characteristically or representatively American in some literary respect, our actual practice suggests that "American literature" really means nothing more than *those few works of fiction, poetry, and drama which have been written in any place that is now part of the United States or by anyone who has ever lived in one of those places and which now rank among the acknowledged masterpieces of Western writing.*

II

The question is, how well does the body of material covered by this implicit definition serve our common ambition to identify the peculiar character of American literature? It seems to me that we could hardly have hit upon a definition less suited to this purpose. By restricting our attention to works written in English and then calling these works American, we simultaneously make American literature a branch of English literature, set ourselves the nearly hopeless task of distinguishing it from English literature, and deny ourselves access to all of those American works in other languages that might enable us to draw such distinctions. By identifying America with the United States, similarly, we forgo any possibility of comparing the developments of English, French, Spanish, and Portuguese literatures in the New World, although some knowledge of these parallel developments would seem indispensable to our expressed aim of measuring the impact that America has had upon literature.

When we go on to construe the United States to mean any place that now lies within its borders, we necessarily distort the tiny portion of American colonial literature we do study, removing it from the America in which it was written and reading it in the light of events that took place many years, sometimes centuries, later. Proceeding on this logic, we read works from those British colonies that eventually became the United States but nothing from the equal number that did not, although the political lines that now separate these places did not exist at the time the works were written, although some of the colonies that we include had more in common with some that we exclude than they did with those that later became their political bedfellows, and although some of the excluded colonies were far more important to the British-American enterprise than were any of the included ones.

Even from a strictly "American" point of view, this retroactive political distinction seems calculated to frustrate any attempt to identify something literarily American. It confers nominal literary citizenship upon every Virginian, even those who thought of themselves as Englishmen, considered Virginia an English colony, and regarded England as their true home; while it automatically denies this ostensible privilege to every Jamaican, including those who considered themselves Americans and America their proper home. Combined with our linguistic stipulation, this political criterion of Americanness obviously excludes all French, Spanish, Portuguese, and Dutch settlers, even though many of them may have felt quite at home in the New World, for all we know. But even without the linguistic rider, the equation of Americanness with residence in a politically defined place manages to dismiss out of hand the entire literature of presettlement exploration in all languages—English among them—although a number of these narratives clearly express the writer's feeling that his experiences in America have radically altered his status, his character, his most fundamental beliefs, his very identity, in fact, and that his new self is linked inextricably to the new world of his adventures.

If our linguistic-political definition of "America" has limited and distorted the materials available for the study of American literature, our belletristic-aesthetic conception of "literature" simply compounds the problem. Insofar as we have accepted without question the idea that fiction, poetry, and drama are the only truly literary forms and that only the best poems, short stories, novels, and plays are worth studying, we have allowed our data to be selected for us by theories that, whatever their critical benefits, have nothing to do with the problem of defining American literature. Mistaking Eliot's distinction between literature and "another thing" as a reference to the proper objects of literary study rather than to its proper methods, we consign to the historians and sociologists large quantities of writing that, if subjected to disciplined literary analysis, just might tell us something about the distinctive shapes that literature has taken in America.

Although our feelings of cultural uniqueness persuade us that American literature is different, it seems, our cultural paranoia forces us to prove that American literature is just as good as European literature, in exactly the same ways, and hence to concentrate our efforts upon the very works that, in measuring up to transnational standards, may well be our least distinctive productions. But even if *Moby-Dick* were the most uniquely American work in our literature, that fact would be incidental to the genre and the artistic virtues of Melville's book. Since neither the novel nor great writing is peculiar to America, these categories cannot help to identify works from which inferences about the Americanness of our literature can be drawn.

Taken together, our operating differentiae—linguistic, political, belletristic, and aesthetic—betray our most fundamental and most questionable assumption: that any excellent poem, play, novel, or short story written in any place that is now part of the United States or by anyone who has ever lived in one of those places must also be American in some deeper sense and that these accidentally American works will reveal their essential Americanness if we will only read them carefully enough. The net effect of this unspoken assumption has been to make the bulk of our study, teaching, and writing (at least insofar as it purports to say anything about American literature) little more than an exercise in question begging. Instead of trying to find out what is American by examining many works that may be American and comparing them with other works that cannot possibly be American, we choose a few works (or allow them to be chosen for us) on the quite arbitrary basis of their language and provenance and on the altogether irrelevant basis of their genre and literary quality, assume that those traits make them American, and then try to decide what is American about them. It is as if we had selected some gray rocks, on the assumption that God made the gray ones, and then studied them to find out if God is really as rich as we have always believed. Having selected from all of the available evidence a handful of texts for qualities that have no necessary bearing on what we hope to discover, we read them over and over again in an attempt to detect in them some common idea, myth, style, form, psychosis, or vision that, once found, we will feel perfectly justified in calling American because it appears in a number of works that we have already assumed to be American.

It is safe to say that nothing very significant or even very interesting can come out of this activity. The works we have chosen can tell us something about themselves and even something about other works that meet the same criteria but nothing necessarily about works in other genres, works written in the United States in other languages, or works written in English outside the present boundaries of the United States, although any number of these may be American in some more essential aspect. What we learn from our chosen works, furthermore, will not necessarily be unique even to themselves, let alone to American literature at large. The materials we study already represent a definition of American literature and cannot lead us beyond it except on wings of fancy.

One might feel less uneasy about this notion of American literature if it did not attract to the field so many graduate students who find the Renaissance or Victorian periods too large to manage; if it did not produce so much repetitious commentary on a few shopworn topics; if it did not persuade us to ignore so much writing that is germane to our professed interests; if it did not send so many potentially able young Americanists off into modernism and the half-worlds of American studies, popular culture, and ethnic studies in search of something new to read and say; if it did not make our enterprise seem so hard to justify in a time of shrinking budgets and withdrawing professional opportunities— if, in short, it did not enable us to do so little while professing to do so much. The evidence, however, is all against us. Although a disproportionate number of graduate students in English have specialized in American literature during the past twenty years, many major universities are unable to find qualified people to fill the chairs in American literature vacated by recent retirements. Each successive issue of *American Literary Scholarship* reviews more and more books and articles to the tune of louder and louder complaints about their lack of originality, learning, and consequence. In the meantime, we grow sour and cynical about the whole point and purpose of our collective enterprise, even as we prepare yet another course on "American Poetry," another article on *Moby Dick,* another book on "The American Novel," another graduate student for a Ph.D. in "American Literature."

III

How did we get into this impossible situation? Although the path that terminates in our present cul-de-sac can be traced back to the earliest debates over the question of a national literature, its fatal turning came at that moment, early in the twentieth century, when American literature ceased to be a predominately journalistic issue and became an academic enterprise, when the magazine editors stopped saying what American literature ought to be and the professors started explaining what it is. The linguistic, political, belletristic, and aesthetic criteria that now define American literature all arise from this event.

Our linguistic bias is perhaps the easiest to explain and the hardest to defend. The academic study of American literature began in departments of English in universities that had themselves been founded to help realize the antique dream of America as the manifest destiny of Anglo-Saxon progress. Of course, mass immigration had long since made nonsense of that cultural fantasy by the time the American Literature Section of the Modern Language Association was organized in 1930, and subsequent changes in academic demography have further obliterated the fancied equation of things American with things WASP. Nevertheless, in continuing to restrict our attention to works written in English, we are still allowing our subject to be defined for us by assumptions we would blush to own.

To a considerable extent, our habits of identifying America with the United States and of conferring retroactive statehood upon the thirteen colonies arise from the same provincial (not to say racist) notion that the progress of Anglo-Saxon culture forms the armature of New World history. Proceeding on this notion, we regard the citizens of other New World nations as authentic Americans only insofar as they profess an affection for our political, social, and economic institutions; while we regard as our forefathers a group of British subjects who not only did not sire us but would certainly disown us if they had. At the time when the subject of American literature was aborning in our universities, this Anglo-Saxon myth of America's historical mission was gathering unwonted support from the United States' recent successful intervention in World War I. Appearing to validate the nation's long-felt and often-proclaimed but hitherto imperfectly demonstrated claims to cultural uniqueness, this sudden translation into international prominence demanded the recovery, or discovery, or invention of an appropriately unique and distinguished American literature. What this uniquely American literature would be, of course, was already determined by its having been born in departments of English to anglophile parents who had themselves been raised in the religion of Anglo-Saxon progress.

Having received its linguistic and political traits at birth, American literature acquired its belletristic and aesthetic character from the changing academic environment in which it grew up. How thoroughly that environment changed and how deeply those changes have affected our conception of American literature may be discerned in the striking differences between the school that governed the academic study of American literature in its early years and the one that has come to dominate that study since 1950. For purposes of identification (and to avoid the pointless quarrel over which is the more scholarly) we may call the earlier school Historical, the later one Critical. These labels are apt insofar as they connect the two schools with their respective *magistri:* Taine and Arnold; designate the models for their respective forms of discourse: historiography and aesthetics; and characterize such examplars of the two schools as V. L. Parrington on the one hand and D. H. Lawrence on the other.

The terms are somewhat less useful in identifying the more fundamental differences between these two scholarly persuasions, especially the political and temperamental biases of which their scholarly interests and methods are largely a reflection. The Historical school selected its tools and its materials in a spirit of progressive liberalism, at a time when American history, if viewed from a sufficiently privileged height, could be construed as having reached a rather advanced stage in its long westward trek out of European captivity into the promised land of freedom, prosperity, and power. American literature, accordingly, was to document a parallel movement out from under the shadow of European "romanticism," through the "rise of realism," into the light of common day.

The Critical school, on the other hand, emerged in a period of spreading uncertainty about the value, if not the reality, of political, social, and material progress in America. Where the optimistic Historians had seen occasional prophetic glimmerings of realism amid the early romantic gloom and a radiant dawning after the Civil War, the more skeptical Critics saw a few redeeming spots of romantic darkness scattered throughout an otherwise unrelieved blaze of official sunshine. Replacing Jefferson with Marx and Freud as their tutelary spirits, the Critics found the real America not in its smiling scenes but in its haunted minds, in a few neglected or misunderstood writers who said, "No in thunder," and in the power of blackness. Where the literary histories had been encyclopedic and impressionistic, criticism became selective and analytic, concentrating its attention upon works that would repay an interest in poetic technique, a taste for deep meanings, and a bias toward doubt and disillusionment. Melville replaced Howells; Poe thrust out Bryant. Figures too large to be muscled aside were reinterpreted. The author of *The Innocents Abroad* became identified with *The Mysterious Stranger,* and the comic ending of *Huckleberry Finn* became a failure of tragic nerve. Hester supplanted Dimmesdale as Hawthorne's alter ego in *The Scarlet Letter.* Whitman became known as the author of *Democratic Vistas* and "Out of the Cradle," and even Emerson's center of gravity shifted from freedom toward fate and the house of pain.

For a number of complicated reasons, many of them sociological, the Critics gradually usurped the posts of academic power and influence once held by the Historians. The pedagogical and literary benefits produced by this palace revolution are well known, and its detrimental effects have been fully itemized by aggrieved

Historians. What concerns us at this point is the severe diminution of materials considered relevant to American literary study that attended the triumph of the Critical school. In 1934, Arthur Hobson Quinn's *American Fiction* traced the historical rise of realism through the artistically uneven work of 113 American novelists. Twenty-three years later, Richard Chase could feel perfectly justified in resting his counterproposition—that the American novel is not realistic at all but a romance—upon a detailed analysis of less than a dozen novels of demonstrable literary merit. There is no denying that the naive historicism and undiscriminating impressionism of Quinn's encyclopedic survey make Chase's close and imaginative readings seem serious and even scholarly in comparison. The point remains, however, that in the movement from History to Criticism little or nothing has been added to our understanding of what American literature is in fact, while large amounts of material that might assist such an understanding have been lost. If the Historians tended to include in their studies whatever seemed to them American and to consider it excellent by definition, the Critics merely reversed the formula, treating only those works that seemed to them excellent and taking the Americanness of those masterpieces for granted.

Had the shift from historical to critical methods occurred at some other time, its consequences might have remained what the Critics intended: a correction of the literary abuses perpetrated in the name of historical scholarship and a reinterpretation of our literary past in the light of a literary present that simply would not fit into any pattern of American progress and had consequently eluded the grasp of the few historians whom it did not merely offend or bemuse. Occurring when it did, however, during a period of unprecedented academic growth, the widespread adoption of critical methods and criteria had the unfortunate effect of narrowing the range of materials pertinent to the study of American literature at the very time when more and more people were beginning to study it. Since World War II, the number of students, courses, advanced degrees, faculty, and publications in American literature has risen precipitously, while the number of works comprised by the subject has declined proportionately. Each year we have said more and more about less and less, until we now find ourselves left with a half-dozen masterpieces and nothing more to say about them.

IV

How do we get out of this unproductive and demoralizing situation? There is no question that we need to. The close critical study of our literary masterworks in isolation may have been desirable, even necessary, twenty-five years ago, but that procedure has long since reached a point of diminishing returns. This is not to suggest, by any means, that nothing remains to be said about these great books, only that nothing new is likely to be said about them as long as we continue to treat them solely in relation to each other. And even if these scholarly considerations were not a sufficient reason for redirecting our energies, recent cutbacks in academic publishing, especially in literary criticism, ought to convince us that the upcoming generation of Americanists will have to find new ways to demonstrate their qualifications for tenure. For reasons of both scholarly principle and professional expediency, we need to redefine the subject we call American literature.

Since the severe restriction of literary interests that led to our present conception of American literature happened to coincide with the rapid expansion of our academic establishment, the recent decline in our institutional fortunes may be taken to recommend an expansion of our interests. Certain peripheral developments in American literary study, begun in the time of our greatest affluence, seem to me incompletely successful attempts to effect just such an expansion. The Popular Culture movement has thrown aside the aesthetic test for allowable materials in order to study some of our less excellent (and hence, the theory goes, more representative) literary productions. For a number of years now, programs in American studies have ignored the belletristic test in order to examine many forms of writing for signs of Americanness. And certain minor branches of ethnic studies have even tried to break the linguistic barrier in order to include in American literature a work or two in some language other than English. But even when these efforts at expanding our subject have not been hampered by academic paranoia, by methodological uncertainty, or by a tendency to confuse literary issues with political grievances, they have still tended to evade the main question—what is American?—by assuming that the materials studied must be uniquely or typically American merely because they were produced in the United States.

Nevertheless, such movements do point a way out of our self-impoverishment: back through those linguistic, political, belle-tristic, and aesthetic codicils to an untrammeled definition of American literature. If we could give up the idea that American literature is written only in English, our subject would immediately include the best poems, fiction, and plays written in all languages in places now lying within our borders or by people who have lived in those places. That in itself would be a significant addition, for it would allow us to stop chatting airily about the "immigrant experience" and to start analyzing and comparing the developments undergone by many imported literary languages and forms as they struggled to accommodate unconventional subjects in a new world. We know, for example, that there are perhaps two hundred Scandinavian novels dealing with the American experience of their foreign-born writers. Thanks to such scholars as Henry Pochmann, E. L. Tinker, Stanley Williams, Olga Peragallo, and Irving Howe, we have varying amounts of information about the German, French, Spanish, Italian, Yiddish, and Hebrew writings produced by the inhabitants of those cultural islands that dot our English-speaking sea. But few of us have read in these known literatures as often as we have reread *The Deerslayer,* and we have not even begun to catalog what has been written in the United States by immigrants from China, Japan, Southeast Asia, or the Middle East.

If we would then abandon our habit of equating America with

places that are now part of the United States, we could study critically praiseworthy poems, fiction, and plays written anywhere in
the New World since the discovery. The main effect of this en-
largement of our subject would be to extend the baseline from
which we are attempting to fix the exact location of that deceptive
isle we call literary Americanness. First of all, by taking the discovery rather than the first British settlements as our starting point,
we gain access to an American literature that is much older than
the one we now study. In 1585, when a hundred British colonists
were starving in caves on Roanoke Island, three hundred American poets were competing for a prize in Mexico City. And second,
by admitting to our studies the development of French, Spanish,
and Portuguese literatures in the New World, we simultaneously
expand the range of literary forms and conventions we can examine for the possible effects of importation into the New World and
provide ourselves with several literary genealogies to set against
the one that now occupies our exclusive attention. How many of
us can say with any assurance that our understanding of the American epic in English, from *The Columbiad* to the *Cantos,* has nothing to gain from what our colleagues in the Romance languages
can teach us about the American epic in Spanish, from Ercilla's *La
araucana* to Neruda's *Canto genéral?* But we need not go even this
far afield to find scholarly reasons for expanding our literary geography. By removing the British colonies from the United States
and restoring them to the world in which they actually existed, we
might resuscitate the whole subject of the literature of British
America and, with the assistance of such catalogs as R. E. Wat-
ters's checklist of Canadian literature and Frank Cundall's bibliographies of West Indian writings, enrich the context in which we
interpret the poems of Anne Bradstreet and Ebenezer Cooke.

If we then went on—or rather, back—and construed "literature," as the old *Cambridge History* did, to mean all forms of written expression, American literature would include distinguished
New World writing in any form and any language. This interpretation of literature seems to me to require far less justification than

does the one we now employ. Letters, diaries, memoirs, histories, polemical and devotional writings are all conventional forms with their own characteristic assumptions and literary strategies, and hence their own possibilities for literary innovation. The boundaries we now draw between fiction and "nonfiction," artifact and "usifact," did not exist in most of the periods we study. Why we continue to insist upon them in the present age of generic confoundment remains a mystery. Travel narratives like *Two Years Before the Mast* and novels like *Moby-Dick* may end up in different sections of the library, but they emerged from the undifferentiated literary experience of people who read, and often wrote, both forms. And although Josiah Royce's *The Problem of Christianity* may not qualify as fiction, its governing metaphors have a great deal to tell us both about the literary backgrounds of Royce's argument and about the religious problem of *The Scarlet Letter.*

Finally, if we remove the stipulation that only acknowledged masterworks are worth studying, we get an American literature that includes all New World writings, whatever their language, form, or degree of artistry. The works that pour in upon our attention when this last critical barrier is knocked away will not necessarily assuage our pangs of cultural inadequacy. But they can become instruments of knowledge if we approach them in a scholarly spirit of curiosity, and they will be good in exact proportion to our ability to make them interesting. If it is truly our ambition to find out what makes American literature unique, and we are not just looking for American works that hold up their heads abroad, then we will read Royall Tyler's *The Algerine Captive* and Freneau's "The American Village" without minding that these works will not bear aesthetic comparison with *Robinson Crusoe* and "The Deserted Village," let along with *Tom Jones* and *The Prelude,* for we will understand that their imperfections can tell us something about the difficulties of fitting American materials into European forms that we cannot learn from the excellence of *Walden* and *Song of Myself.*

Without even considering all of those European works, from

More's *Utopia* to Rimbaud's *Le Bateau ivre* and beyond, that have been directly influenced by American writing, then, we have managed in a few strokes to expand the contents of American literature a thousandfold. When the phrase "American literature" is stripped of its acquired qualifications, the word "American" signifies everything having to do with civilization in the New World since the European discovery, and "literature" includes every written document that will respond to literary analysis. Here is a vast landscape indeed—one fully commensurate to our capacity for belief in the nobility, complexity, and uniqueness of American literature. The American literature embraced by this definition is nearly five hundred years old. It is written in many languages, and it comes from many places scattered throughout a world whose size, shape, and meaning have changed continually since 1500 because America was discovered. Confronted by a prospect at once so exhilarating and so intimidating, we may perhaps be pardoned if, like Columbus at the mouth of the Orinoco River, we feel initially less inclined to plunge ahead than to withdraw into the safer confines of our old world-picture.

On the other hand, we do not have Columbus's excuse for preferring the theories of Isidore, Bede, and Strabo to the wonders he beheld with his own eyes. For our New World, unlike his, is by no means unexplored; it is simply unknown to most of us, the professors of American literature. Leaving aside the extensive available scholarship on such topics as the development of Spanish, French, and Portuguese literatures of Europe, we may notice the work of Thomas H. Adams and his staff of bibliographers at the John Carter Brown Library. Building upon catalogs compiled over the last four centuries by such scholars as Possevino, Sabin, Medina, Borba de Moraes, Vail, Harrisse, Pollard and Redgrave, Wing, Evans, and Shaw and Shoemaker, Adams's staff is attempting to assemble a reasonably complete listing of American documents in five categories: "obvious Americana" (books concerned entirely or primarily with the New World), "lost Americana" (similar books of which no copy has survived), "partial Americana" (publications in which America is a subordinate topic), "inferential Americana" (works in which no specific reference to America appears but which took the form they did because America was discovered), and "iconographical Americana" (maps and prints). This omnium-gatherum already includes well over a quarter of a million items, and new titles are being added every day.

What are we to do with a subject of this magnitude? First of all, as Adams's project amply demonstrates, the literature must be brought under some measure of bibliographical control: identified, located, attributed, dated, and described. Once we have some idea of what the subject contains, these contents will have to be arranged taxonomically—by language, provenance, genre, period, subject, and technique—so that they can be treated historically. When this necessary groundwork is done, perhaps we can begin to make some tentative propositions regarding the subject as whole. In the meantime, we must begin to prepare a generation of scholars for the tasks ahead by making sure that our graduate students receive the kind of training in languages, bibliography, research, and literary analysis that the study of American literature demands. These students will have to understand from the outset what the field comprises so that they will enter it with no misapprehensions regarding its scope or the possibilities of mastering it and so that they will have some idea about where their own scholarly projects fit into the topic at large.

Clearly, anyone who aspires to profess American literature thus defined has his work cut out for him. But what about those of us who find the subject quite rich enough as it is presently constituted? What options remain to present Americanists who feel themselves either unfitted by training or disinclined by scholarly interest to start all over again in a wholly new and extremely demanding field? The redefinition I have produced does not mean that what we presently call American literature is not a subject. It implies only that this subject is not American literature. Those of us who choose to go on teaching and writing about U.S. literary classics in English should at least advertise our offerings accurately. If, for example, instead of calling our usual first course "Early American Literature" or "Colonial American Literature," we were to call it "The Literature of British America," that simple change of titles might remind our students, and ourselves, that the British colonists did not live in the United States, that British America also included islands in the Caribbean and parts of present-day Canada, and that there is in the same period a literature of French America, of Spanish America, of Portuguese America, and of Dutch America—literatures that are no less American for not having been written in English. And if, by the same token, we would call our traditional second course "Masterpieces of U.S. Literature in English," we might remember that the assigned readings reflect our critical tastes more than they do our understanding of what is American, that the literature of the United States has been written in many languages, and that the United States is not the only American nation with a literature worth studying.

In addition, such simple retitlings might remind us that the works now taught and studied under the rubric of American literature exist in contexts other than the one they form among themselves. As masterpieces, they should be studied alongside the classics of other literatures. Having been written in English, they should be read in connection with English literature. As poems, novels, or plays, they belong to a genre; and as products of a certain time, they belong to a period in literary history. Observations about their subjects, themes, and techniques similarly must be made, not on the assumption that these details are representative of, or unique to, the culture in which the works were written but in the light of some wider knowledge about the employment of analogous subjects, themes, and techniques in other literatures.

Most important of all, perhaps, by refusing to call our present subject American Literature we may dissuade ourselves and our students from making statements about American literature on the basis of a few works whose evidential value is slight at best. And this self-restraint might serve continually to remind us of all of the available evidence upon which such statements might be based, should anyone feel emboldened to make them. The literature of the United States in English is an American literature, to be sure, and ought to be studied as one. It is, however, only part of American literature in English, which is in turn only one of many American literatures, each of which has something important to tell us about American literature as a whole. Like America itself, which began to be discovered only when Europeans came to realize that they really knew nothing about it, American literature will remain a terra incognita until we are ready to admit that it is neither the earthly paradise nor the howling wilderness of our provincial imaginings but a strange new world where, as Columbus put it, "The farther one goes, the more one learns."

Discovering the Literature
of British America

Those of us who plow the hard ground of early American liter-ature have grown accustomed to hearing certain charges flung at us from the richer adjacent fields of the English Enlightenment and the American Renaissance. There is precious little early Amer-ican writing, say our more fortunate neighbors, and what little there is, is either not very literary or not very good. When it isn't utilitarian and didactic, it is merely derivative, which is to say un-American. Consequently, the only reason for studying it is that it foreshadows, either directly or obversely, the truly literary and truly American masterpieces of the nineteenth century. In the view of our colleagues and even our own students, it seems, we are "bent resolutely on wringing lilies from the acorn."

This proud contumely might be easier to bear if we were readier to refute it—if, in fact, we did not harbor among our most shame-ful secrets the uncomfortable feeling that these judgments are cor-rect, that early American literature really isn't—can't be—a liter-ary subject in the same sense that nineteenth-century American literature is, and that unless we want to spend our time making either excuses or ridiculous claims for a handful of generally medi-ocre poems, we must be content to rustle the dry bones of history and theology. Only within our own little freemasonry, it seems, can we call our materials "literature" and our studies "literary" without raising hoots of derision. And even in this cloistered sanc-tum, the words ring untrue against our memory of mighty lines from *Paradise Lost,* "Windsor Forest," and *Moby-Dick.* It is hard to avoid the suspicion that, like the Plymouth Pilgrims themselves, we chose this stony soil not for its riches but because no one else wanted it.

Granted, this puts the case against early American literature in its harshest terms, and, like all worst cases, this one slights the very real contributions that a number of scholars have made to the literary content and reputation of the field. Still, there is enough truth in the indictment to suggest that our image wants repair and that, insofar as we concur in the judgments against us, the repair must begin with our image of ourselves, our materials, and our methods. Until we purge our own suspicion that there isn't much early American writing, that most of it isn't literature, that none of it is very good, that it is important mainly in relation to what comes later, and that its overall character is already well known, we can hardly expect anyone else—even other Americanists—to think better of our subject.

Since the unflattering reputation of early American literature rests on these notions, we might begin the process of renovation by examining them individually in some detail. The widespread belief that the field is small has managed to resist every effort to dispel it. To cite only one case among hundreds: in 1944, Harold Jantz attempted to correct the general misapprehension that early American poetry consists entirely of the work of Anne Bradstreet, Michael Wigglesworth, and Edward Taylor by listing the poems of 164 New England writers of the seventeenth century and by outlining the contexts in which these poems are to be understood and appreciated. Almost a quarter-century later, however, the history of American poetry, according to Hyatt Waggoner, still began with Bradstreet, Wigglesworth, and Taylor. That Jantz doesn't figure in Waggoner's historical calculations may of course be due to the omission of *The First Century of New-England Verse* from the standard bibliography of American literature, but that omission simply confirms what Waggoner's study implies: the historians of American literature will maintain their illusion of the early period as a thinly populated landscape despite our persistent attempts to correct it.

On the other hand, our own tacit acceptance of this notion may have made us less imaginative and industrious than we might be in developing the resources of early American literature that do

exist. Of the work done in the field each year, certainly far more is
devoted to reinterpreting, according to the latest critical fashion,
the relatively small canon of well-established and often-studied
texts than to expanding the list of texts available for study. Even
Early American Literature is forced by its contributors to publish twenty articles on Cotton Mather, Benjamin Franklin, and
Charles Brockden Brown for every report on some hitherto unknown text. This situation would be bad enough in a field where
the existing materials had been largely cataloged and examined. It
is simply inexcusable in early American literature, where the number of unexamined documents exceeds the number of familiar
texts ten-thousandfold. To my own very incomplete knowledge,
there are in print at least six hundred bibliographies and catalogs
listing pieces of early American writing. Identified in these bibliographies are tens of thousands of documents, in print and in
manuscript, deposited in libraries and archives throughout the
English-speaking world. Closer at hand, there are at least two
hundred published collections of these materials, some containing
many volumes, all in modern, easily accessible editions. Furthermore, because these lists and collections have come to my attention as the result of a very cursory search through the most familiar bibliographical guides, I am certain that even this vast store of
early American writing constitutes only a portion of what in fact
exists.

But is it literature? The answer to that question depends entirely
on our definition of "literature." Even if we take this word, in its
old generic sense, to mean belles lettres—poetry, fiction, plays,
and what used to be called the "familiar essay"—a good deal of it
will almost certainly turn out to qualify. But if we define "literature" in its more modern, functional sense as any piece of writing
that employs literary techniques and, consequently, will respond
to literary analysis, then the supply is limited only by our store of
analytic methods. Franklin's *Autobiography* wasn't born with the
strawberry mark of literary nobility on its shoulder blade; it became literature, as *Pamela* did, by being treated literarily. Every

piece of writing contains information that only literary analysis can extract, and its value as a literary work depends entirely on the amount of information it can be made to divulge by these means. *Hamlet* is better than *Pamela* because more literary scholars have been able to say more interesting things about it. In other words, the amount and quality of early American literature depends finally upon ourselves. For anyone who doubts this proposition, the possibilities for making literature out of nonbelletristic materials, and the methods of doing so, are amply demonstrated in the work of such scholars as Hayden White and David Levin on historiography, James Russel Hart and James L. Clifford on biography, Daniel Shea and Robert Sayre on autobiography, John Seelye and Wayne Franklin on travel writing, Sacvan Bercovitch and Emory Elliot on sermons and polemics, Gordon Haight on letters, Stephen Kagle on diaries, Howard Mumford Jones on promotional tracts, Roy Harvey Pearce and Richard Van Der Beets on captivity narratives, Kenneth Lynn on journalism, Gary Wills on state papers, and, of course, Roland Barthes on everything from magazine advertisements to guidebooks. Our ground is not barren; it only wants literary cultivation.

That the field has not been better cultivated is due largely to the notion that early American literature owes its significance to what came later, that Hawthorne alone makes John Winthrop worth the attention of literary scholars. This idea of the seventeenth and eighteenth centuries as a tail wagged by a nineteenth-century dog arises partly from the identification of literature with belles lettres. If literature means poetry, fiction, and drama (itself a nineteenth-century idea), and if colonial America produced little or nothing in these forms, then most writings of the period can be admitted to the salons of literary study only on the arm of some later work of art. Those seventeenth- and eighteenth-century writings that cannot attach themselves to *The Scarlet Letter* or "Hamatreya" must remain outside on the street, a prey to cruising historians. The main source of this retrospectivism, however, lies in the origins of our subject itself. Just as the popular interest in colonial

American history arose in the nineteenth century from nationalistic motives, to affirm the political and cultural identity of the United States by giving it a purely "American" genesis, the academic study of early American literature emerged in this century to help justify the separation of American from English literature by creating a native tradition for our national treasures. Like Freneau, who located the spiritual roots of the American village in the domestic affections of the Indians, scholars of American literature have viewed the colonial period mainly as the seedbed of some later flowering rather than as a subject in its own right.

As a result of this Whig historicism and nationalistic mythmaking, early American literature has always been, in effect, a nineteenth-century subject. Puritanism has been confounded with the metaphorical uses that were made of it in the nineteenth century, as an image of social repression or a golden age of belief or America's dark ages. Typologists turn out to be latent symbolists, antinomians become incipient romantics, while figures who cannot be made into forebears of the nineteenth century are largely ignored. Viewed from this side of the Revolution, British America loses its own historical and geographical character and takes on a nineteenth-century shape. Instead of nearly thirty British colonies, stretching from the Arctic to the Amazon, with Barbados and Virginia the most highly prized and New England considered the least important among them, we see only the thirteen colonies that became the United States, with New England at their center, Virginia on the periphery, and Barbados nowhere in sight. Given our idea of America as a nation that emerged in the nineteenth century, of American literature as a collection of national masterpieces written in the nineteenth century, and of our own subject as an early stage of these political and literary developments, the wonder is not that early American literature has failed to become a subject in its own right but that it has managed to attract any serious attention at all. How many Milton scholars would there be if that seventeenth-century Puritan were read only in the light cast back upon him by Blake and Wordsworth?

Although one feels embarrassed to say anything so obvious, the fact is that pre-Revolutionary American writing can have nothing to do, immediately, with the United States, with the shape and meaning of North America in the nineteenth century, or with *Leaves of Grass,* unless, like some of the writers we study, we wish to argue that all of these things exist together in some eternal plan of human history. Otherwise, these writings must be seen to have arisen from, and to refer to, a situation of their own: the extension of British culture into the New World and the resulting impact of this extension on that culture. The world that produced these writings and is reflected in them has a shape and meaning of its own. It is, first of all, much larger than the original United States, for it includes Newfoundland, Guiana, Virginia, Bermuda, Plymouth, the Amazon, Nova Scotia, Barbados and St. Kitts, Massachusetts Bay, the Leeward Islands, Quebec, Providence Island, Maryland, Connecticut, New Hampshire, Maine, Rhode Island, Jamaica, Carolina, New York, New Jersey, Hudson's Bay, Pennsylvania, Georgia, Montreal, and consolidated Canada. At the same time, the British American's world was much smaller than, say, Jefferson's or Melville's. The charter for New Haven granted that colony a tract of land extending along the coast for one hundred miles and inland, for a supposedly equivalent distance, to the Pacific Ocean. Most important, this world changed its size and shape continually over the years between the first plantings and the Revolution, as a result both of the activities reported in contemporary writings and of the writings themselves.

Considered in relation to this world, rather than to that of the nineteenth century or to ours, early American writing becomes a very different subject. Like British America before the Revolution, it is much larger than we have normally assumed. Like the map on which New Haven was planted, it has its own peculiar shape and meaning, not those we have imposed upon it in retrospect. Like New World geography before the expedition of Lewis and Clark, it changes shape continually as time goes on, continually altering the context in which its elements have their mean-

ing. And like Barbados and New England in the colonial scheme,
its most and least important works are not necessarily the ones
identified by later developments. So different is this subject—in
its size, shape, essential nature, and scale of values—from the one
we have inherited, and so incompletely studied is it, that our received opinions concerning the general character, the major figures, and the main tendencies of early American literature are, if
not totally uninformed, at least seriously premature. Before we
can even presume to make general statements about this enormous and largely unread body of material, we have a great deal of
work to do.

To begin with, the subject needs to be defined in its own terms,
according to its own peculiar situation, rather than in relation to
American literature as a whole, whose center of gravity lies outside our period, in a significantly different world. Instead of calling our subject Early American Literature or Colonial American
Literature—thus defining it from the outset as a prelude to something else—we had better call it the Literature of British America,
which is to say: literature written in English before 1765 by persons
who spent some time in the New World. By *literature,* I mean not
just belles lettres but any piece of writing that can be subjected to
literary analysis—can be *used* as literature. The specification that
this literature be *written in English* simultaneously conforms to the
customary subclassification of literatures by language (German,
French, Russian), respects the essential importance of language in
the formation of the character of any literature, avoids the confusion and special pleading that arise when we try to subclassify
literature along political or geographical lines (British, American),
tacitly acknowledges the existence of American literature in languages other than English (French, Dutch, Spanish, Portuguese),
and, not least, recognizes that our subject is studied almost entirely in departments of English.

By further stipulating a literature written in English *before 1765,*
this definition observes the dividing line, long maintained by British Imperial historians, between the "Old Empire" that preceded

the Stamp Act Congress and the "New Empire" that followed it. Although this act of rebellion directly affected only the thirteen continental colonies, it transformed the whole character of British America by abruptly changing both Britain's attitudes toward all of its colonies and the attitude of the colonies toward themselves. By virtue of this single event, we may say, the world that both generated and was created by British-American writing gave way to an altogether different one.

The subject is limited, finally, to literature written in English before 1765 *by persons who had spent some time in the New World,* in order to fence off what would otherwise be a bewilderingly amorphous field. Although somewhat arbitrary, the delimitation seems more reasonable than one that would include only writings *about* America, or works *published in* America, or something of the sort, which might well exclude many works written by English-speaking people who spent their whole lives in the New World. And while this differentia unfortunately excludes works by people like More, Shakespeare, Marvell, and Donne, it does manage to include a number of works not normally thought of as belonging to our subject; like Aphra Behn's *Oroonoko.* But even more important, this criterion recognizes a fundamental distinction between a writer's immediate experience of a place (however linguistically conditioned that experience may be) and the impressions that writers receive from printed sources.

The virtues of this definition seem to me very considerable. First of all, it permits us to decide whether or not a given work belongs to the literature of British America before we interpret it. Whereas a piece of Early American Literature must be shown to be an early case of literary Americanness before it can be included in that subject, works in our subject are identified solely by language, date, authorship, and susceptibility to literary analysis. Second, because the definition presupposes nothing further about the works it identifies—that they are typically "American" or "tradition directed" or whatever—the category remains independent of whatever we may say about its contents. Such statements as

"Early American Literature is conditioned by the proximity of the frontier" identify the works they describe and are therefore tautologies. Propositions regarding the literature of British America, on the other hand, can be disproved because they refer to a body of writings previously established and agreed upon. Third, the subject thus defined has its own identity, apart from the formation of the United States or the publication of "The American Scholar," or the creation of the American Literature Section of the MLA. As a result, we can think about what our own writers were doing and why, without feeling continually obliged to account somehow for what Thoreau or Faulkner would do centuries later. At the same time, the literature of British America as we have defined it is a logical subcategory of a larger subject: American literature in English after 1765; which is in turn part of an even larger subject: American literature in all languages since the discovery of the New World. Our subject can therefore be compared with the literature of French America and the literature of Spanish America—the colonial components of American literature in those languages—and can thus contribute to a theory of American literature as a whole, a theory of the impact that America has made on literature.

To define our subject as the Literature of British America—writings in English before 1765 by persons who had been to the New World—is to lay out for ourselves a very large scholarly project. First of all, we must bring the subject under some measure of bibliographic control by identifying those materials that fit the definition. Once those documents have been listed and located, each one must be analyzed and described in relation to the several contexts—literary, linguistic, biographical, historical, and geographical—implied in the definition that enabled us to identify it. What is its genre, its topic or theme, its structure, and its style? To what other works do these qualities relate it? Where does it stand both in the historical development of the language and on the linguistic map (both regional and social) of its own time? How does it compare with other British American writings of its time and with those written in its particular region of British America over time? And where does it fit into the life and oeuvre of its author? Each of these questions establishes an interpretive context, a body of primary materials in relation to which the document in question can be read, understood, and explained. Equally important, each question identifies the secondary, scholarly works that will provide the information we need to answer it. The literature of British America includes many thousands of documents, each of which is related, in various ways, to hundreds of other primary works, within the field and outside it, and thus to topics that have been dealt with by generations of scholars in scores of secondary works—all in all, a subject of truly vast proportions.

Daunting as it may seem, the scholarly task imposed by our definition of the literature of British America is perfectly clear. We have invented a subject in order to discover it and must now get on with the work of discovery. For the teacher, however, the Literature of British America poses a special problem. Given a standard anthology of colonial American literature and a roomful of students willing to be persuaded that Edward Taylor begat Emily Dickinson, we know exactly what to do. But how do we teach a subject that is largely unknown, whose contents, shape, and meaning have yet to be discovered? We can hardly declare a moratorium on the subject until we ourselves have mastered it. If my estimate of the territory ahead is even roughly accurate, the final conquest is a long way off and will require the efforts of scholars who must be recruited from the ranks of today's students. Therein, I think, lies the answer to our pedagogical problem. Instead of merely reporting to our students the results of our discoveries, we must train them to become discoverers themselves.

To illustrate the sort of training students need for this work, and some of the direct benefits they can derive from it, I want to describe very briefly a graduate seminar in the Literature of British America that I have been conducting over the past two or three years. Unlike most courses in literature, this one has no syllabus of required readings selected from an established canon to convey the instructor's opinions about the subject. Instead, it offers a sequence of exercises designed to acquaint students with the problems of formulating topics for literary research and the methods of pursuing that research. The seminar begins with a meeting or two in which we first examine the structure of traditional studies in colonial American literature and its underlying assumptions and then redefine the subject along the lines laid down in this essay. Armed with this new definition of the materials that belong to the subject, we then confront the problems of identifying and locating these materials.

What we need is a complete list of extant documents composed in English before 1765 by persons who had been to the New World. Since there is, so far as I know, no list of this sort, it must be compiled from existing partial lists—those that deal with only part of the subject (part of British America, say, or only part of the period, or only one of the written forms we have decided to include), those that subsume all or part of the subject within some larger subject (English imprints before 1800, for example, or books about America in several languages), and such specialized lists as catalogs of physical collections that appear to include relevant works. To find out what lists are available in these various categories, we need another list, a complete bibliography of published bibliographies, which again does not exist and must be compiled from partial lists of various sorts (universal and special, closed and serial). To learn what bibliographies of bibliographies there are, we must consult yet another collection of partial lists, those general and special guides to reference materials that, being listed nowhere but in each other, must be sought out in the library.

The students' first task, accordingly, is to prepare a list of those guides that, together, will give them access to all of the relevant bibliographies of bibliographies. In order to determine the usefulness of the guides they uncover, we first prepare a working outline of topics—under such headings as Subject Areas (humanities, social sciences, etc.), Geographical Areas (America, the British Empire, etc.), and Historical Movements (European expansion, the discovery and settlement of the New World, etc.)—that pertain to our subject and at least one of which should be covered in the guides we eventually select. When each student has prepared a tentative list of potentially useful guides, they all meet to compile a single list of the most useful, least redundant titles and designate one of their number to present that list, in the form of a critical report, at our next weekly meeting. After hearing that report and filling in what seem to me any important lacunae, I assign one of these guides to each student and ask him or her to extract from it the titles of all of those bibliographies of bibliographies that appear to contain lists of primary and secondary works that belong to our subject. When the students have assembled these individual lists, they again meet to cull out duplicate titles and prepare a single list, on which one of them will report at our next meeting.

The former process is then repeated. Each student is assigned one bibliography of bibliographies and asked to extract from it all bibliographies containing primary works that promise to fit our definition of the literature of British America. From their individual lists of primary bibliographies, the students formulate a single, final list of titles and present it in class. This card file is, of course, by no means complete, since they have examined only a few of the sources at each level. Although a class of six students will turn up thirty or forty guides to research materials, they will actually work with only a half-dozen of these. And of the one hundred or so bibliographies of bibliographies they find in these guides, they will again use only six to identify potentially relevant primary bibliographies. Even so, the results can be astonishing. A single class, starting from scratch, will end up with around three hundred primary bibliographies. And if each new class is presented with the findings of its predecessors and asked to expand rather than to replicate the list, another 150 primary bibliographies can be added to the store every time the course is offered. Consequently, even though no class ever comes close to completing the task all by itself, what they are able to do gives them a clear sense of how large the subject is as well as a set of procedures for dealing with it.

Having learned to identify materials that belong to their subject, the students are now introduced to the methods of locating what they have identified. In a single meeting, we survey the various catalogs that enable them to find a known document (book, periodical, or manuscript) in their own library, in local research libraries, in American libraries generally, and in European libraries and archives. The aim here is to acquaint students with the principal finding aids for their own library (the card catalog and those for periodicals, documents, manuscripts, special collections, and microfilms) and also with some (printed catalogs, guides to special collections of books and manuscripts, computer catalogs, and catalogs of microforms) that give researchers access through their own libraries to libraries elsewhere.

Each student is now asked to select, from the primary bibliographies we have found, one document that fits our definition of the literature of British America, to locate that document, and to write a seminar paper about it. Meanwhile, in order to consider some of the necessities and possibilities for these papers, we all read one work—a captivity narrative, say, or a promotional tract—and meet to discuss the sort of paper one might write about it. Examining this text carefully, we attempt to define, first, the various contexts—literary, linguistic, historical, biographical, and geographical—that it implies; second, the sorts of information one would need to understand these contexts; and third, the sorts of secondary works that would provide this information. Equipped with some sense of what they are looking for, the students return to our list of bibliographies of bibliographies to compile a list of major secondary bibliographies that identify scholarly writings on these subjects.

After a meeting devoted to compiling a single list of these secondary bibliographies and discussing some of the problems of locating and evaluating secondary materials, the students are ready to begin work on their papers. As a first step, each student is asked to prepare a prospectus, including a description of the document selected (its form, subject, author, date, situation, provenance, and style); an outline of the information one would need to account for these attributes; and a working bibliography of secondary materials likely to provide this information. These prospectuses are presented individually and discussed in a series of seminar meetings, enabling the students to clarify their topics, to share bibliographical information, and to expand their common store of analytic techniques. The students then go off to finish their papers, meeting individually with me once or twice a week to settle particular problems. Before the date on which each paper is scheduled for discussion, the writer provides every member of the class with a copy so that everyone can read it ahead of time and come to class prepared to ask questions about it. If, after hearing these questions, the writer feels that the paper can be significantly improved, he or she may revise it before submitting the final draft for a grade.

It may be said, not unjustly, that for a course in the literature of British America, this one exposes students directly to very little of that literature. A class of six will actually study only seven primary works; and even if these happen to represent different genres, periods, and geographical areas, they will hardly provide an overview of this enormous field. What the students do get, however, seems to me much more useful and much more pertinent to the subject in its present condition than any survey of preselected works could possibly be. First of all, they learn some fundamental methods of literary scholarship that will enable them to study this subject (or for that matter, any other subject) on their own: how to define a field of study; how to identify and locate primary materials in the field, how to describe, analyze, and interpret nonbelletristic writings; how to identify, locate, evaluate, and use secondary materials; and how to report the results of research and analysis. What is more, because students who sign up for this seminar are presumably interested in the subject and because the study of the subject requires these methods, the students really do learn them, as they seldom do in graduate courses in bibliography, where scholarly procedure tends to be taught in a vacuum, apart from its motivating object. Scholarly research is not incidental to this subject, something done a long time ago by people who dug up the works that students are now expected to read. It *is* the subject. Studying the literature of British America means finding out what it is and what can be said about it.

As a result, what students do in this course is not essentially different from what a veteran scholar in the field must do. Whereas the study of Shakespeare or the American novel or the Puritans presents the graduate student with an established canon of texts and a mountain of published opinion regarding those texts, the literature of British America presents a problem and a set of necessary tasks. By performing those tasks, students become immediately engaged in the scholarly activity that constitutes the subject. Instead of performing exercises that merely imitate or replicate what has already been done, they can actually add to existing knowledge. By selecting from the thousands of available texts works that are seldom read and on which little or nothing has been written, they can very quickly become *the* authorities on those works. They come to know things that no other literary scholar has ever known. Because the information they gather can be fundamental and still be original, when they come to report what they have learned, they can avoid all of those self-serving tactics—the bumptious disparagement of established authorities, the overstatement of niggling points, the dogged prosecution of bizarre interpretations—by which graduate students attempt to clear a little space for themselves in overcrowded fields.

This sense of authority that comes with the chance to do genuine, original scholarship has an additional benefit. Whereas the student who writes on William Byrd tends to avoid the published scholarship and criticism because it seems to leave so little of consequence for a beginner to say, those who study the literature of British America develop a positive hunger for secondary works. Left on their own with some largely unstudied work in a largely unsanctified genre, they quickly discover that to say something defensible, significant, and interesting about that work they need information—about its form, its language, its author, its geographical and historical situation. These documents raise questions that must be answered before the documents can be explained, interpreted. To the student who has no questions, the library looks like an unnavigable sea of ink. But those who know what they need to know can identify the secondary works that are most likely to answer their questions and then choose the ones that answer them best.

From the instructor's point of view, perhaps the most agreeable consequence of these procedures is that the papers tend to be more professional, readable, informative, and above all more *interesting* than such apprentice exercises usually are—far more so, at any rate, than one more reading of "Hasty Pudding," one more interpretation of Jonathan Edwards as a crypto-Transcendentalist, or one more poorly equipped expedition into John Cotton's theological maze. Realizing that any example in cases like this can be a two-edged sword, I might mention a few of the essays I have received over the past couple of years: an examination of Robert Hunter's *Androboros* (1714) in the context of Augustan political satire, Restoration comedy, the burlesque tradition, New York politics, and Governor Hunter's literary and administrative career; a history of the 150-year metamorphosis, from catechism to primer, of Cotton's *Spiritual Milk for Babes* in the light of contemporaneous changes in educational theory and in children's literature; an explanation of the curious mixture of Edenic and Infernal materials in Lionel Wafer's *A New Voyage and Description of the Isthmus of America* (1969) as resulting from its having been written originally in the conventions of the buccaneer narrative and then turned into a promotional tract for the Darien Company; a study of Samuel Sewall's *The Selling of Joseph* (1700) in relation to Puritan biblical theology, earlier antislavery tracts by Quakers, pamphlet literature in general, published responses to Sewall's tract, his other writings on the problem, and later antislavery works; and, finally, an investigation of the authorship of *The Life and Adventures of Bampfylde-Moore Carew* (1745), attempting to determine whether the writer had in fact been to America, as he claims, and hence whether the work meets all of the requirements for inclusion in the literature of British America.

But surely the most beneficial result of this approach, for instructor and student alike, is an awakened sense of how large, how fertile, and how untouched this despised field of ours really is. The possibilities it offers for significant, original research seem to me nearly limitless. What remains, in Caribbean and British archives, of the writing done in the heyday of the Barbados colony, not only by the planters—who were born and educated in England, thought of themselves as exiled Britons, sent their children home to school, and returned there themselves the minute their tour of duty was finished—but also by the overseers, literate, English-speaking Americans who were born and buried in the New World? What literary relations, if any, existed among Britain's far-flung American colonies—in Canada, New England, the middle-Atlantic coast, the continental South, and the Caribbean—and how did these relations complement or complicate those between individual colonies and the mother country? Was written English changed in any significant way, between the discovery and the later eighteenth century, as a result of the struggles by British explorers and settlers to describe and explain their unprecedented experiences? What forms of writing did they adapt or invent to express their radically changing conceptions of the world and of their place in it? How did these linguistic and formal innovations affect the character and the development of English literature as a whole? Who were the major figures in this movement, the original, influential geniuses? And which, of the thousands and thousands of documents that make up the literature of British America, are its classics, at once representative and uniquely distinguished? Back beyond the Declaration of Independence, off the Boston Post Road of provincial American literary history that runs through our anthologies, there's a whole new world of English literature just waiting to be discovered.

The Earliest American Novel:
Aphra Behn's Oroonoko

I

Why is *Oroonoko* never included in studies of the American novel or in courses on Early American literature? As a literary work written in English about America by someone who claims to have lived there, it would seem to deserve a place in the canon at least as much as, say, John Smith's *Generall Historie,* a work that few Americanists would think of ignoring, even though Smith was not an American and his narrative is not exactly "literature." To be sure, *Oroonoko* was not written in America, but then neither were most of Franklin's *Memoirs, The Prairie, The Marble Faun,* and *The American.* Nor was it written for Americans and published in America, but neither were Nathaniel Ward's *Simple Cobler of Aggawam* and Crèvecoeur's *Letters from an American Farmer.* And we certainly do not exclude *Oroonoko* because Aphra Behn was not an American citizen or because she was born in Europe and died there, for on those grounds we would also have to strike from our syllabi all American writings before 1776, as well as the works of such migrants as Henry James, Vladimir Nabokov, and Gertrude Stein.

So far as I can see, the only possible reason for the omission of *Oroonoko* from American literature is that Surinam, the scene of the action and the place of Aphra Behn's putative American residence, is not a part of the present United States—or as Howard Mumford Jones used to call it, "the future United States."[1] But this criterion makes very little sense. In the first place, it lacks any historical meaning, inasmuch the United States did not exist prior to the Declaration of Independence and therefore cannot reasonably be thought to have conditioned anything done in America before that time—unless, of course, like the "Early Americans" themselves, we are prepared to argue that events widely separated in time all exist together in a single, eternal plan of human history. Otherwise, we must regard the America to which writings like *Oroonoko* relate as the one that existed at the time they were written. And that America, as even the most cursory glance at any seventeenth-century map will show, was a very different place—in size, in shape, and in meaning—from the one that existed in the nineteenth century, when nationalist historians began to take a patriotic interest in the "colonial backgrounds" of the United States, and from the one we know today.

In 1688, when Aphra Behn wrote *Oroonoko,* not all of the thirteen rebel colonies yet existed; and those that did belonged to a much larger political entity called British America, which extended, at one time or another in its history, from the Arctic Circle to the Amazon and included Surinam. In another respect, Aphra Behn's America was much smaller than Jefferson's or Moses Coit Tyler's; her contemporaries in New Haven fully expected to discover the South Sea within a hundred miles to the west of their settlement. Nor were the relations among Britain's American colonies anything like what is implied by the idea of a "future United States." Virginia and Carolina had far more in common with the Caribbean colonies than with Massachusetts Bay or Connecticut, while each individual colony was apt to be in closer touch with England than with any other part of British America. And although nationalistic literary historians have taught us to consider New England the most important of Britain's American territories, that preeminence in fact belonged to Barbados in the seventeenth century, with New England near the bottom of the list.

If, as a criterion for identifying works of early American literature, the concept of "the future United States" is unhistorical, it is also unliterary, in that it does not designate some literary feature that is common or unique to works written in that place. Of course, had Aphra Behn lived in Connecticut, some Americanist would have forged a set of native literary credentials for *Oroonoko* by now, by tying it thematically, formally, spiritually, or however to some acknowledged masterpiece of fiction written in the

United States a century or more later, just as D. H. Dickason sought to naturalize William Williams's *Mr. Penrose* by finding in that delightful novel foreshadowings of *Moby-Dick*.[2] If these attempts to Americanize *Oroonoko* by association had failed, as Dickason's efforts on behalf of *Mr. Penrose* seem to have, then neither the retroactive citizenship granted to its author nor its own literariness would have prevented it from being left off the list of required readings in American literature. Although Richard Lewis lived in Maryland and wrote what has been called "the best neoclassical poem of colonial America,"[3] our inability to think of "A Journey from Patapsco to Annapolis" as a "future *Song of Myself*" has kept the poem out of the history of American literature. But even if Aphra Behn had lived in New England and we were able to discover some literary resemblance between *Oroonoko* and, say, *Huckleberry Finn,* we would still not be justified in calling this common literary feature "American" except on the untenable assumption that whatever one finds in two or more works written by sometime residents of places now part of the United States must itself be "American."

The questions raised by *Oroonoko* suggest that we need a better way to identify works of American literature—better, that is, than by merely determining that the author was, according to some elastic political definition, an American, that the work in question conforms to our current notions of literature, and that it bears some resemblance to certain other literary works written by Americans. Since Americans have produced literary works of almost every conceivable stripe, including a good many that no one would think of calling "American," and since those so-called American features that recur in the classic works of notable American writers can also be found in works written by non-Americans, authorial nationality does not seem to constitute a necessary condition of American literature. *America* is a place. *Literature* is a kind of writing. If *American literature* is to mean something more than all of the literature ever written in that place—if, in other words, it is to denote a literature that is identifiably American—

it must establish some necessary relation between that place and that literature, one that will give the word "American" a literary meaning.

On what grounds might such a relation rest? Since "America" designates a place, its literary meaning must have to do, somehow, with the appearance of that place in literature. Should American literature, then, comprise all of those literary works in which America is mentioned? No one, I imagine, would say so. Subjects do not in themselves constitute literary properties or adequately define literary kinds—*Rasselas* is not an Abyssinian novel. In any case, literature *about* America is no more what we have in mind when we speak of American literature than is literature *in* America. On the contrary, what we are looking for is America in literature. But since America, as a place, has no inherent literary meaning of its own, it can acquire literary meaning only by taking on a literary form. To enter literature on a truly literary footing, America must make a difference in the way literature is written—which is to say, in its selection, deployment, and arrangement of words. By the same token, to be considered literarily American, and not just politically or geographically so, a work must be seen to take linguistic cognizance of America, incorporating some idea of that place into its very form of words. If we can locate somewhere a literary work whose form can be attributed directly to the impact of America on the written language, then, no matter where we find it or who wrote it, we can say that we have discovered a literature that deserves to be called American.

II

Reading *Oroonoko,* as we necessarily do, in the light of all of the prose fiction produced over the last three centuries, we tend automatically to think of Behn's work as a novel and then, with *Clarissa* and *Moby-Dick* and *Ulysses* in mind, to dismiss it as a very imperfect example of the genre. Although perhaps unavoidable, this ahistorical view begs its own question: Why should we so readily attach the name "novel" to a work written at a time when the various things we understand by that word—the form itself, the world it describes, its peculiar language, the readership to whom it speaks—did not yet exist, were only in the process, so to speak, of being invented? When, "never rest[ing] my Pen a Moment for Thought," Behn composed her history of the Royal Slave, she was not trying to write a novel and failing. As one of the newly emerging class of professional writers created by the decline of aristocratic patronage after the English civil war and the rise of a new audience of book buyers, she was simply trying to earn a living by composing, from the literary materials available to her, a story that this as yet ill-defined readership would buy and praise because it portrayed a world they recognized.

In one respect, Behn was unusually well equipped for her task. Her pen had supported her reasonably well for nearly twenty years, and she had worked successfully in virtually every important genre of her time except the epic. For the Restoration theater she had composed heroic dramas, romantic tragicomedies, comedies of wit, of intrigue, and of manners, farces, pastorals, masques, operas, and at least one tragedy. Forced by changes in the political, economic, and social climate to seek support in the popular marketplace, she had turned in recent years to writing those varieties of prose entertainment that her contemporaries lumped together under the name of "fiction": epistolary romances, novellas, Italian romances, French Arcadian romances, romantic tales, and translations of moral maxims and popular scientific treatises from the French. Alert to sources of income in every level of her society, she had also produced celebratory odes for the royal family, lyrics and verse narratives dedicated to courtiers and to influential members of the professions, and anthologies of poetry for the commercial market. She was an accomplished professional who knew what would sell and how to write it.

In almost every other respect, however, she was singularly ill-prepared for her assault on the common reader. Although her own pedigree is obscure, she was apparently reared and educated among the landed gentry, and she identified herself always with the titled classes, professing an unswerving devotion to the Stuart monarchy in the very face of its imminent collapse. She was an unreconstructed Tory and an avowed Catholic in a society whose tolerance for such recherché attitudes was growing slimmer by the day. Worse yet, she was a social rebel whose undisguised hatred for the legal institution of marriage and allegiance to the authority of disinterested love were mistaken by her aristocratic friends and middle-class enemies alike for libertinism. It was a romantic ideal of natural love that she celebrated in her plays, not sexual license. But the attitude toward conventional morality and the behavior arising from that attitude were not always distinguishable from those routinely displayed in the Restoration theater. And if the court had called her plays salacious simply because they were written by a woman, what sort of reception could she expect in the city, whose denizens she had repeatedly portrayed as joyless, puritanical hypocrites undone by witty, amorous cavaliers?

Behn's is the classic case of the modern professional writer, schooled in a lofty ideal of truth and art and forced by mundane circumstance to make her living in a world that she disdained and that held her ideals in contempt. That her personal vision of the good as a Tory Arcadia ruled by peaceful shepherd kings was a nostalgic fiction, hopelessly out of touch with modern history, is nothing to the point. Unless she simply abandoned that vision, she would have to find some way to bridge the gulf between her feudal paradise and the progressive "new England" of her intended audience. Had she been merely a hack, unhampered by allegiances of her own, she could have manufactured tales of honest apprentices, religious romances, or antiromantic burlesques as effortlessly as she had churned out satires on the Parliamentarians or congratulatory poems to the several monarchs who occupied the English throne in rapid succession during the 1680s. In that case, *Oroonoko* would have been a very different book, and we would not be scratching our heads over it today, for it would have disappeared from sight along with *The City Heiress, The Amours of Philander and Sylvia,* and *A Voyage to the Isle of Love.* Because she was motivated by personal conviction as well as by necessity, however, she sought to make a place for her antique ideals in the hated modern world. Out of that quixotic ambition, she produced a book so remarkable that it has rescued the rest of her oeuvre from oblivion and seems now, for all its stumbling oddity, to anticipate the whole subsequent history of English fiction.

The strategy Behn devised to reconcile the conflicting demands of personal inclination and public taste is, on the face of it, ingeniously simple. She merely fashioned a romantic tale of highborn lovers caught in the cross-currents of desire and duty and then presented this old story in the very modern guise of a Brief True Relation of her own travels to America. This conflation of Old World and New World genres seems to have suited her purposes exactly. On the one hand, the prose romance was in every sense her métier. Not only was she thoroughly practiced in its conventions, having read romances all of her life and modeled most of her plays (to say nothing of her own behavior) upon them, but like most persons of her class and education, she regarded them as accurate pictures of reality and as dramatizations of her own most cherished values. The Brief True Relation, on the other hand, simultaneously evaded her busy middle-class readers' distrust of idle fictions and met their demands for useful information about current affairs in brief compass. What is more, because the Brief True Relation rested the authority of its statements upon the writer's experience, rather than upon his or her social station or sex, the form allowed Behn to assume an authority that had been begrudged her in the masculine, courtly domains of drama and poetry. And because the experiences reported in these narratives of New World travel were necessarily unverifiable, the form permitted her to call her tale a true history without fear of rebuttal. By enfolding her romance of the Royal Slave in a Brief True Relation, Behn could stick to her romantic last, proffer her fiction as news from the New World, and thus foist it upon the very audience whose members were busily dismantling the world that the romance had been devised to validate.

To say that Behn wished to make a place for romance in a new world is true in more than just a commercial sense. She was not simply trying to peddle an old product in a new market; she wished to discover in the prosaic and turbulent modern world that history was constructing about her a place where the vanishing ideals embodied in romance could survive the predations of change and even rise again to regulate human society. To Behn, as to many another European who lamented the passing of traditional ways and the decline of civil order in the seventeenth century, America seemed a place out of time, where man's original estate might be regained. Ever since the discovery, narratives of New World travel had couched their actions in the tropes of chivalric romance and described America in images of the Earthly Paradise, the Garden of Eden, and the Golden Age.[4] If the discovery, exploration, and settlement of America formed an inextricable part of that historical change that had removed humankind from its primal condition, then by casting themselves upon this historical tide men might hope to complete the circular course of human history, arrive again at the beginning, and remain in that perfected state forever. For Behn, America embodied an ideal condition of feminine nature, the original kingdom of love from which men fell into history when they took up the masculine pursuits of war and commerce. Transported there by masculine desires for glory and wealth, the loving woman and bellicose male of romantic tradition might be reconciled in a perfect, eternal marriage. For such a redeeming expedition from the Old World to the New, the narrative form of the Brief True Relation, even though it was devised to take hold of the most world-shaking event in modern history, might well seem the speediest craft.

The vessel is fairly launched with the narrator's opening announcement that the story to follow is a true "History," rather than the "Adventures of a feign'd *Hero,* whose Life and Fortunes Fancy may manage at the Poet's Pleasure." Although it will prove as "diverting" as any fictional romance, like all such reports by plain-speaking voyagers, "it shall come simply into the World," without the adornments of artistic "Invention," recommended solely "by its own proper Merits, and natural Intrigues." The truth upon which its charm depends, moreover, will lie not in the familiarity of its details or its conformity with recognized conventions but in the narrator's own experience. "I was myself an Eye-witness to a great Part of what you will find here set down," the narrator maintains, "and what I cou'd not be Witness of, I receiv'd from the Mouth of the chief Actor in this History, the *Hero* himself." Addressing her busy reader, who has not the leisure demanded by the conventional, multivolume romance, she then explains that she has omitted, "for Brevity's sake, a thousand little Accidents of [the hero's] life, which . . . might prove tedious and heavy to my Reader, in a World where he finds Diversions for every Minute, new and strange."[5] And to inspire the confidence of this apparently preoccupied and literal-minded reader, she precedes the introduction of her hero with a circumstantial account of the slave economy, flora, fauna, and native inhabitants of Surinam, couching these data all the while in images of the Golden Age—of innocent, free Indians who live, like "Adam and Eve," without either shame or immodesty, codified laws or organized religion, "Curiosity" or "Fraud," "Vice or Cunning" (131–32)—those images that had recommended America to Behn as the ideal setting for a New World romance.

That Behn regarded the Brief True Relation primarily as a vehicle for her romance is evident in the dispatch with which the narrator abandons that modern conveyance, after five pages, and turns her attention to its precious Old World cargo. The next thirty-odd pages, nearly half of the complete text, are devoted to Oroonoko's life in the court of Coramantien and his rivalry with the king, his grandfather, for the hand of Imoinda. Taken straight from the English heroic drama and the French Arcadian romance, and offered here as an account given to the narrator by Oroonoko after his arrival in Surinam, this familiar story of conflicting romantic principles employs none of the narrative techniques introduced in the opening relation. The narrator is now undramatized and omniscient, a teller of someone else's tale and, like her reader, an audience to that tale, rather than a particular person reporting her own observations in a particular place. Indeed, the narrator does not even take care to report only those things that Oroonoko, her supposed source of information, could have seen at the time or learned about subsequently. Romantic actions happen objectively, in the eternal order of things, and do not depend for their existence, as the recently discovered and ever-expanding New World did, upon the perceptions of individual human beings. The value of these actions lies not in their individual contributions to the accumulating store of human knowledge about the world but in their coherent moral structure, which imitates the divinely instituted form of the world and of human history.

Unlike the structure of the Brief True Relation, which arises from a sequence of actions performed by an observing, reflecting individual on the ground, that of the romance precedes its action as an empty form into which details of various sorts, from the most realistic to the most fantastic, can be poured and thus given a familiar valuation. In broad outline, this form comprises an initial situation, a conflict arising from (or introduced into) that situation, a series of complications that elucidate both the conflict and the particular virtues required to overcome it, and a resolution that serves to confirm those virtues and to create a final situation that demands no further action. Because these virtues are of the highest sort, the action is performed by noble characters; and because these noble actions have universal meaning, their physical setting in any particular instance remains a matter of virtual indifference, a mere backdrop against which the moral drama is played out. Nowhere in Oroonoko's African adventures do we find anything resembling the narrator's earlier interest in the topography, economy, botany, and zoology of Surinam and its closely related anthropology. Behn's readers have often observed that the African court of Coramantien bears a striking resemblance to the courts of Europe. The point is, rather, that the story of Oroonoko and Imoinda told thus far, being a romance, could happen anywhere without affecting its form one whit.

Since the romantic conflict of this story pits Oroonoko's love for Imoinda against his duty to the king, who wants her for his harem, it projects a resolution in the form of a wedding between the lovers and a resolution with their monarchical parent. Nothing irremediable appears to lie in the way of such a resolution. The king has violated the local taboo against a father's coveting his son's intended bride, and Oroonoko has retaliated by breaking the corresponding taboo against a son's meddling with one of his father's chosen wives. But these transgressions do not seem to be fatal. No one has been killed or cursed, and Imoinda has not been physically dishonored; so the way to sanity and bliss still lies open. To be sure, the king sells Imoinda into slavery after discovering her midnight tryst with Oroonoko. But Oroonoko himself is captured by a slaver very soon thereafter, and if the lovers don't know that they are bound for the same place, the experienced reader of romances certainly does. Apparently, the conflicts and divisions that have arisen in the Old World and, with the transportation of the two lovers, have become insoluble there are to be repaired in that innocent, aboriginal America to which we were introduced in the opening description of Surinam. As Oroonoko says upon disembarking from the ship that has brought him to America, *"Come, my Fellow-Slaves, let us descend, and see if we can meet with more Honour and Honesty in the next World we shall touch upon"* (166–67).

The reader's expectations of a happy resolution to the romantic conflict are seemingly vindicated in the events that follow quickly upon Oroonoko's landing in the colony. He is immediately recognized as a king, given the name of "Caesar," greeted by the loyal colonists as if "the King himself (God bless him) had come ashore," and "received more like a Governor than a slave" (169). In addition to the customary freight of heroic virtues, it appears, Oroonoko comes bearing his creator's loyalty to the beleaguered Stuarts and her fond if unsubstantiated hopes for their permanent restoration to power over an obedient, orderly realm. While the local slaves, many of whom are Oroonoko's own former captives, prostrate themselves before him, "crying out ... *Long live, O*

King!" and paying him "even Divine Homage" (170), Trefry, his new owner, treats him "as his dearest Brother," lodges him in his own house rather than among the common slaves, and promises "on his Word and Honour" as a gentleman to return the prince to Africa (168). At a great feast staged in Oroonoko's honor by the slaves, Trefry tells him about a recently arrived beauty named Clemene, who turns out, of course, to be Imoinda; and within three pages the lovers are reunited, wed, and expecting a child. For the happy conclusion of the romance, only the rupture between these lovers and the old king of Coramantien remains to be healed; and as anyone familiar with the genre would know, such problems are easily dispatched. Whether Oroonoko and his gravid spouse return to the welcome of a once tyrannical parent now softened by remorse, or the king conveniently dies during their absence, or they decide to remain in America and establish a peaceful dynasty of commingled love and honor in that regained paradise, the romantic action has virtually arrived at its projected conclusion.

At this point, however, the action takes an unexpected and decidedly unromantic turn. Oroonoko is still a slave and cannot be freed until a new governor arrives from England to replace the previous one, the narrator's father, who has drowned at sea in a hurricane. True, Oroonoko suffers "no more of Slave but the Name" (169–70), and his aristocratic friends at Parham House have promised to secure his freedom. Nonetheless, "Caesar" is a slave name in fact and a royal title only in a fictional sense—in another world, as it were. Nor is the English colony populated solely by aristocrats of the sort who rule the world of romance. During this interregnum, the real power lies in the hands of ambitious upstarts and wealthy hoodlums like Byam and Banister, "such notorious Villains as *Newgate* never transported," who cannot be expected to assist the designs of a romantic action because they "understood neither the Laws of God or Man, and had no sort of Principles." (200). These uncultivated renegades, Oroonoko fears, will never let him go, for his title and noble bearing only make them detest him the more, while his wife and expected child triple his value in the slave economy. As a slave, Oroonoko has neither love, since his wife and child don't belong to him, nor honor, since his present safety and eventual liberation depend on his lying low at Parham house, showing no signs of restiveness until the new governor arrives. If he attempts to secure his love and regain his honor by inciting a slave rebellion, Imoinda will become Byam's hostage, and his friends among the aristocratic planters will be forced to side with the overseer class against him.

Oroonoko's entanglement in the intractable circumstances of colonial politics, economics, and class conflict alters the tone and import of the narrative markedly. We seem to have moved without warning from that morally translucent world where "Heaven was so kind to the Prince as to sweeten his Misfortunes by so lucky an Accident" as his reunion with Imoinda (173–74) to an altogether different sort of world, one governed by untidy historical conditions rather than by universal principles of love and honor. These unlooked-for complications follow so closely upon Oroonoko's arrival in the New World that a devout Americanist might be tempted to ascribe them directly to the change of geographical venue from Africa to America, on the assumption that America is, after all, a very special sort of place. The fact is, however, that life in seventeenth-century Coramantien was obviously no less subject than Surinam to such historical conditions; while Surinam, as the opening pages of "Oroonoko" demonstrate, was no less susceptible than Coramantien to romantic treatment. The crucial change, in other words, is formal and stylistic. It occurs at the point where the action departs from the timeless circle of romance form and enters the historical form of the Brief True Relation for the first time. In the opening four or five pages of the text, we heard the beginnings of Behn's Brief True Relation of life in Surinam, without Oroonoko. The succeeding forty pages gave us the romance of Oroonoko and Imoinda in Coramantien, outside both Surinam and the narrator's own immediate experience. Now, with only a third of the volume remaining in the reader's right hand and the action seemingly poised for its final sprint to a happy conclusion, Oroonoko finds himself in a strange new world, created by conflicting human desires rather than by divine intentions, where nothing is conclusive but death.

In calling her tale a "History," Behn appears to have intended only to imply that it actually happened and thus to lull the philistine prejudices of her middle-class reader. In adopting for this purpose the narrative form of the Brief True Relation, however, she was in effect subscribing to, and subjecting her hero to, a radically modern idea of what "history" means. Because the Brief True Relation was devised specifically to report observed conditions in a new world that had first come to light as a direct result of present human enterprise rather than through knowledge transmitted from the distant past, and because that world grew larger with each effort to encompass it, the form portrayed human action in terms of an unfolding geography and this expanding landscape in terms of a corresponding change in the character and attitudes of the traveler.[6] In the romance, as in medieval historiography, the chronology of events is not conditioned by geography, which serves merely as a backdrop for the exemplary actions of exemplary figures who, being motivated by universal moral principles, do not change significantly in the course of the action. In the Brief True Relation, on the other hand, human action and geographical situation are mutually conditioning elements in the historical evolution—the creation—of reality. Geography and chronology, Richard Hakluyt proclaimed, are "the right eye and the left eye of all history." History without geography, John Smith agreed, "wandreth as a vagrant without certaine habitation"[7]—thus denying at a stroke the belief held by medieval historian and romancer alike that human history has its home in the divine mind, in the eternal plan of redemption, and locating that history squarely in the evolving individual soul.

Behn's investment of her romantic action in this narrative form generates a sequence of events and a level of discourse somewhere between fiction and history, whose import can only be called novelistic. While Oroonoko continues to pursue the goals of love and honor set for him in the romance of Coramantien, he must do so through an ever thickening jungle of bureaucratic delays, demeaning expediencies, political rivalries, and geographical circumstances. Born with "a Spirit all rough and fierce.that could not be tam'd to lazy Rest" (176), he is yet obliged to spend his time entertaining the narrator with tales of his former exploits and listening to "all the pretty Works" in her repertoire but avoiding the sort of heroic action that might imperil his and Imoinda's safety and would, in the best possible case, only send him into the wilderness to live like a savage, with no hope of either returning to Coramantien or establishing his dynasty in Surinam. Whatever notions Behn may have held regarding the New World as a theater for heroic actions and a haven for romantic ideals, these fond designs seem to be enmeshed now in a tightening coil of petty, vulgar constraints.

With Oroonoko trapped between unheroic docility and suicidal rebellion, the narrative takes an evasive turn, off the line of fatal action that seems headed for either dishonor or death into a series of diverting adventures in the countryside. By means of this "Digression," which she admits "is a little from my Story" (189), the narrator apparently means to provide her frustrated hero with some opportunities for action that will get him out of the house but will not require the colonists to crush him. In a succession of tall tales, recounted in the purest manner of the Brief True Relation, Oroonoko kills "Tygers," wrestles with an electric eel, and guides the narrator's party to an Indian village, behaving all the while with appropriate bravery and chivalrous concern for his female companions. "Diverting" as they are, however, these exploits merely forestall the inevitable decision Oroonoko must make regarding his dishonorable captivity. What is more, even though his companionship gives the narrator and her friends the heart to venture into the wilderness, his undignified role as a captive entertainer of idle aristocrats robs his heroism of any real consequence. The narrator herself appears to realize the falsity of Oroonoko's position, for he fades from view for long intervals while she describes the local topography and inhabitants, supplanting his actions with her own reflections upon the exotic world that unfolds before her as she penetrates the unexplored wilderness beyond the settlement.

Digressive as it is, this interlude has a profound effect upon the main action. Not only does it demonstrate that Oroonoko's heroism depends on his making the fatal choice between love and honor, but by reemphasizing the narrative methods of the Brief True Relation, it places the narrator at the very center of the action and involves her directly in that choice. Whereas the narrator of a romance stands outside the action, in the presence of the reader, the Brief True Relation places the narrator, who is both the principal actor and the reporter of that action, in the game and out of it at once. What is more, because it is the narrator's experiences that have made him who he is, someone with the authority to speak, he tends quite naturally to identify himself more closely with those experiences than with the untraveled reader. Throughout her first-person report, Behn's narrator has moved back and forth between the familiar English world of her readers and the exotic lands that only she knows, at one moment claiming that since her return to England she has placed certain entymological specimens on display at "his Majesty's *Antiquary's*" (130), where the reader can presumably go and see them; or alluding to well-known historical events, like the Treaty of Breda and the death of Charles II, which have occurred since the putative year of her departure from Surinam; and at another moment referring to Oroonoko in the imperfect tense—"I have often heard him say . . ." (159–60)—as if he were still alive and she were still with him in America. At one point in the narrative, in fact, she manages this temporal and geographical shift in the course of a single sentence, traveling by way of those uncertain pronominal references and unsteady verb tenses that make seventeenth-century English prose such a puzzle for modern readers. Upon first introducing her hero, the narrator addresses her audience on its own English ground: "But before I give you the Story of this *Gallant Slave,* 'tis fit I tell you the Manner of bringing them [i.e., slaves] to these new *Colonies. . . . "* As the sentence continues, however, it abruptly removes the narrator across the Atlantic to Surinam and into the midst of her own narrative: "those [slaves] they [the colonists] make use of there [in Surinam], not being *Natives* of the Place: for those [natives] we [colonists] live with [here in Surinam] in perfect Amity . . . " (129). Drawn by the rhetorical gravity of the Brief True Relation into the action of her tale, the narrator will eventually find herself not merely a witness to its outcome but a principal actor in it.

The final episode in the digressive interlude that lies between Oroonoko's happy marriage and his horrible death takes the narrator and her traveling party to an Indian village upriver, where she undergoes an experience that fixes her more firmly in the New World than anything perhaps except her assumption of responsibility for Oroonoko's safety and liberation. Meeting the Indians, who have never seen a white person before, she immediately becomes conscious of her own strange appearance, as if she were seeing herself through their wondering eyes, and describes herself for the first time. What she sees of herself and her companions from this outlandish point of view is reported in the Indians' words, which, although perfectly innocent, assume in context an ironic edge that is hardly flattering to European assumptions of cultural superiority. *"We shall know Whether these Things can speak,"* the natives exclaim, whether they have "Sense and Wit" and can "talk of Affairs of Life and War," as Indians can (185–86). Like so many New World explorers before her and many more to come, the narrator has been given a new perspective on the world as a whole. Seen from this American coign of vantage, Europe is no longer the center of the circle of lands. It is merely one more place on the globe, as backward in its way as are the barbarous nations in theirs, a relative thing rather than the seat of absolute values by which the rest of the world may be judged. Noting the innocent credulity of the Indians, she quickly realizes that "it were not difficult to establish any unknown or extravagant Religion among them, and to impose any Notions or Fictions upon 'em" (186), a realization that unavoidably includes in the category of

"Fictions" the religion that she and her reader share.[8] It is a vision that, once entertained, can never be thrown off, and it severs the traveler irreparably from the untraveled reader, the very person upon whose sympathy and assent the authority of the narrator ultimately depends. If the effect of the romance is to unite narrator and reader in a world of shared beliefs, that of the Brief True Relation is inevitably to place the narrator in a new and distant land, one that readers can inhabit only by abandoning their own.

Having sought to evade the unpromising drift of her tale by means of the narrative form that caused all of her difficulties in the first place, the narrator returns to her proper "Story" to find nothing changed, except that this story has now become her own—a tale of her increasing departure from the settled moral world of her English readers into the unexplored American wilderness of her own invention. When, weary of prudent inaction, Oroonoko finally rebels against his captors, the narrator finds herself swept up in his mounting hostility to her own kind. Throughout her narrative, she has taken an ambiguous attitude toward her fellow colonists, employing the pronoun "we" to distinguish the white settlers from the Indians and the African slaves but isolating herself by calling the English "they" whenever slavery, especially cruelty to Oroonoko, is the subject. There are, in addition, a number of passages in which the Indians, like Montaigne's cannibals, are depicted as more noble, even more essentially Christian, than their supposedly civilized oppressors. Now, however, all semblance of ambiguity and lofty satire vanishes as the narrator submerges her voice in Oroonoko's, first paraphrasing the harangue by which he stirs up his fellow captives and then modulating into direct quotation as he excoriates all white people for their faithlessness and inhumanity.

Depending on their politics, Behn's readers have taken this speech either as an expression of her own views on slavery or, noting the complacency of the narrator's remarks on the subject elsewhere, as Oroonoko's opinions alone.[9] Both of these readings seem partly right. While Behn appears to have held no very advanced ideas about the evils of slavery itself, it is impossible to

avoid the impression that Oroonoko's diatribe bespeaks her own
suppressed rage against the betrayal of all of those cherished
things that her romantic hero has come to represent. Called "Caesar," he bears a name synonymous with "absolute monarch" in
Behn's time, the one she gives to Charles II in her poem "A Farewell to Celladon on His Going into Ireland" (1684) and to James
II in her *Congratulatory Poem to Her Sacred Majesty Queen Mary,
upon Her Arrival in England* (1689). As a slave, he shares the plight
of women, regarding whom the anonymous author of the *Defense
of the Female Sex* (1696) observed that "like our Negroes in the
western plantations, [they] are born slaves, and live prisoners all
of their lives,"[10] and whom Hippolyta, the betrayed woman in
Behn's play *The Dutch Lover* (1673), compares to "a poor, guilty
slave" who "drags his loathed Fetters after him" (1:273–74). If it
seems strange to think of Behn's presenting her feminist indictment in a masculine voice, we should observe that her preface to
The Lucky Chance (1686) proclaims, "I value Fame as much as if I
had been a *Hero,*" that in the same speech she refers to "the Poet
in me" as "her masculine Part" (3:187), and that in all of the other
fictions she composed during the 1680s Oroonoko's role is taken
by a woman. But, above all, Oroonoko personifies the ideals of
cosmic order, social harmony, and individual nobility embodied
in the romance, ideals that Behn saw being ravaged by modern
history in the world about her and subverted by some implacable
fictive logic in her own narrative.

When, following Oroonoko's inflammatory speech, the narrator resumes her own voice, she adopts a sardonic tone of thinly
disguised hostility that is notably absent from her previous discourse and can only be attributed to her preceding identification
with the rebellious Oroonoko. At the same time, she seems eager
to reestablish contact with her reader and to dissociate herself
from Oroonoko, whose accelerating troubles she feels powerless
to alleviate, even as she feels guilty for having failed him. If
Oroonoko is responsible for the unprecedented passion of her
tone in these concluding episodes, he is also the cause of her efforts to distance herself from him. The grievances aired in his ha-

rangue to the slaves include the complaint that "we are bought and sold like Apes or Monkeys, to be the Sport of Women" (191), which seems to refer to the narrator herself and to those of early days of his captivity when, she says, "we entertain'd him . . . , or rather he us" (177). Once the uprising has begun, moreover, she naturally identifies herself with the white colonists, using the pronoun "we" to denote the common targets of his revenge. In the next moment, however, Oroonoko's enemies become "they," as Byam's vigilantes pursue the fugitive and the narrator stands by powerless to protect him. For the remainder of her story, the narrator shifts her position repeatedly, first aligning herself with Oroonoko's aristocratic friends against his low-life pursuers, then speaking familiarly to the reader as an English author, then dissociating herself from all of the colonists and from the reader as well by referring sarcastically to one timid member of her party as "a bold *Englishman*" (205), then implicitly condemning herself by quoting Oroonoko's charge that all whites are liars, and then ranging herself among the whites by begging Oroonoko's pardon on behalf of his tormentors. But most of all, she vacillates between protestations of her own innocence and apologies for her faint-heartedness, her absence during his capture and execution, her failure to assert her "Authority" (198) on his behalf, and finally, for the inadequacy of tale itself as a fitting tribute to "this great Man" (208).

These rapid shifts in narrative attitude create an ambiguity of tone that enhances the novelistic effects already produced by the collision of Behn's romantic theme with her historical narrative form. Neither romance nor Brief True Relation, her narrative has become a rhetorical blending of heroic ideals and brute reality into a symbolic expression of the narrator's conflicting allegiances to her civilized audience and her savage art. When Oroonoko finally realizes that conditions in Surinam forbid the marriage of love and honor, nature and culture, that he hoped to discover in this "next World," he takes Imoinda into a nearby grove, love's own pastoral domain, and beheads her, thereby removing the impediment to honorable rebellion and, in destroying his wife and unborn child, removing his main reason to rebel at the same time. Unmanned by grief, he mourns over the half-buried body of Imoinda for eight days, until a searching party, attracted to the spot by an egregiously unromantic "Stink that almost struck them dead" (204), discovers him. Thinking to take advantage of his weakness, "the *English*" move to recapture him, whereupon he repulses his enemies by hacking off a piece of his own flesh and throwing it in their faces. This barbarous gesture, learned from the Indian braves he visited during his expedition with the narrator, betrays a striking change in Oroonoko's character, an assimilation to his savage surroundings in preference to the putative civility of his faithless captors and feckless friends. He has gone native, thereby committing the one unpardonable sin available to the missionaries of Old World culture, and insofar as the narrator follows him imaginatively, she must relinquish all claims to her reader's sympathy and trust.

How deeply Oroonoko penetrates into the heart of the savage wilderness and how closely the narrator follows him may be discerned in the powerfully affecting language of the tale's final episode. After some days spent recuperating at Parham House, Oroonoko is abducted by the parvenu rabble and executed. As they slowly dismember him, he stoically smokes an Indian pipe. Before he dies—or "gave up the Ghost," as the text has it—he blesses his executioners. And when he is dead, Byam sends to the plantations, by way of a warning to the other slaves, Oroonoko's quartered remains, the "frightful Spectacles of a mangled King" (208). Amalgamated in this unforgettable tableau are images of all of the hopes that the narrator has invested in her Royal Slave: the natural nobility of the American Indian, the divine right of the martyred Charles, and the redemptive sacrifice of Christ.[11] Having been brought down from the luminous spheres of romantic allegory to the opaque realities of bureaucratic delay, class jealousy, hopeless servitude, and decomposing flesh in the New World, Oroonoko is elevated by his debasement into a complex symbol of Old World hopes aesthetically vindicated in the very moment of their historical extinction.

The closing pages of *Oroonoko* reenact the psychic turmoil of all of those European explorers who came to America armed with Old World ideas about it and then, having undergone experiences that utterly discredited these ideas, found themselves unable either to resume their previous lives at home or to remain isolated in the new world they had discovered. Oroonoko's death constitutes an indictment of everything that Behn's new reader represents—social ambition, commercial enterprise, the subjugation of "dusky tribes," the dismantling of ancient institutions. Insofar as she clings to her hero, acknowledging the savage metaphor of his rebellion and death as her own truest language, she forfeits the support of that audience upon whom all modern writers must depend not only for their livelihood but for their very sense of themselves as writers. Insofar as she distances herself from Oroonoko, however, and aligns herself with her English reader, her tale condemns her as a coward and a liar. The narrator's opening remarks located the value of her tale in its historical truth and the authority for that truth in her own experiences as an American. Later, recognizing the failure of her account to do Oroonoko full justice, she ascribed its deficiencies to that same source: "But his Misfortune was, to fall in an obscure World, that afforded only a Female Pen to celebrate his Fame" (169). Now, in closing, she blames its weaknesses on her lack of artistry, the very feature that she originally offered in evidence of its truth and had advertised in the prologue to *The Young King* (1679) as an American characteristic (2:105). A "more sublime wit" might have succeeded in conveying Oroonoko from his "obscure World" to the new England. As it is, the survival of his "glorious Name . . . to all the Ages" must depend not on the narrator's authority as an American but on the "Reputation of my Pen," the fame she has won in the London theater since her return from the New World (208).

Appearing to recognize that her very dubious reputation as a libertine author of scandalous aristocratic plays will hardly impress her middle-class reader, Behn turns her back upon this audience and, in a dedicatory epistle to Lord Maitland (5:509–11), seeks the protection of a noble patron, a ghost of the old order that died with Oroonoko. Once again, she admits the shortcomings of her book, seemingly equating these with her hero's "Inglorious . . . end" and her own inability to prevent that catastrophe. It is a "true Story": "The Royal Slave I had the Honour to know in my Travels to the other World." Since this world is not further identified, the reader is permitted to think of it both as America and as an imagined country: "If there be anything [in the story, in the place] that seems Romantik [i.e., fictional, untrue] I beseech your Lordship to consider these Countries do, in all things, so differ from ours that they produce unconceivable Wonders, at least so they appear to us, because New and Strange." What happens in that "other World," it appears, is both fictional and true at once, according to a logic that nullifies the author-traveler's intentions. "Though I had none above me in that Country," Behn quite justly insists, "yet I wanted power to preserve this Great man." The problem, she concludes, is a formal one, evidenced in certain "Faults of Connexion" among the various elements of her tale. These faults, however, she now attributes not to her want of "sublime Wit" or to her "Female Pen" but to her headlong, unreflecting methods of composition. "I writ it in a few Hours," she explains, "and never rested my Pen a Moment for Thought." Having embodied her romantic hopes in Oroonoko and then cast him upon the narrative tide of the Brief True Relation, it seems she could only sit and watch him perish. Recounting her early meetings with the Royal Slave, the narrator says, "He call'd [me] his *Great Mistress;* and indeed my Word would go a great Way with him" (176). In the event, his words were to go even farther with her, to an "other World" where English fiction had never been before and from which there was no returning.

III

Conceived as literature written by citizens of the United States or by sometime residents of places now part of the United States, on the deterministic assumption that these conditions produce writing of a uniquely, characteristically American sort, "American literature," must exclude *Oroonoko*. Even if we revise the definition of America to include all of the New World that was known in Aphra Behn's day, her membership in the company of American writers remains in doubt, for it is not at all certain that she ever went to Surinam. Those who believe that she was in fact there take their evidence from *Oroonoko,* from the very equivocal remarks in her dedicatory epistle to Lord Maitland and her prologue to *The Young King,* and from the posthumous biographical sketch of Behn written by "One of the Fair Sex." Those who argue that she never traveled to America, on the other hand, point to the obvious fictionality of *Oroonoko,* the lack of any external support for her claim, the patently commercial designs of the pseudobiography, and, above all, the striking similarities between the descriptions of Surinam in *Oroonoko* and those in such authentic narratives as George Warren's *Description of Surinam* (1667) and Thomas Tryon's *Friendly Advice to the Gentlemen-Planters of the East and West Indies.*[12] If the Americanness of a literary work depends on proof of authorial nationality or residence in the New World, the Americanness of *Oroonoko* must remain in doubt.

But if we define "American literature" in literary rather than in political or geographical terms, as writing conditioned by those linguistic changes that resulted from the transportation of European languages to the New World and from efforts on the part of those languages to apprehend that unprecedented phenomenon,[13] then the Americanness of any literary work has nothing necessarily to do with its author's nationality or place of residence. With the sole exception of the indigenous tongues, all of the languages that American writers have used transcend the geographical and political boundaries of the Western hemisphere and form linguistic worlds of their own. Linguistically united as these worlds are by the circulation of written texts in their respective common tongues, no geographical or political subsector of any linguistic community can remain immune to changes that happen in another. Although the anglophone world contains pockets of mutually unintelligible dialects, the language employed by its literate

population is strikingly uniform, simply because a linguistic vari-
ation introduced into the written language in one place will
spread so quickly throughout the international community of English readers. The idea of an American literature distinct from
British literature was concocted to express political animosities
and is based on the notion that there are two worlds, one Old and
one New. But as the sixteenth-century Spanish writer who called
himself el Inca Garcilaso de la Vega perceived, "There is only one
world, and though we speak of the Old World and the New, this
is because the latter was lately discovered by us, and not because
there are two."[14] While there are reasons for maintaining that
writings in different tongues constitute distinct worlds, no one of
these can be subdivided into an Old World and a New, except at
the historical point where the New World came into being. From
that point on, there is only one world, as Garcilaso rightly observes: the new one that was born with the discovery of America.

Viewed in this light, the vexed question of Behn's American
residence is rendered moot by the fact that to write *Oroonoko* she
employed a narrative form that had been devised specifically to
register those changes in the shape and meaning of the world and
in the concepts of human identity and history that were prompted
by the discovery, exploration, and settlement of America. If she
borrowed from other Brief True Relations, that fact only ties
Oroonoko more firmly to the genre. John Smith's *Generall Historie*
is a virtual anthology of documents written by other explorers.
For the travelers themselves, as for the emerging generation of
modern historians who collected their narratives—Peter Martyr,
Richard Hakluyt, Samuel Purchas—the redaction of existing documents was a perfectly acceptable, even obligatory practice. They
were writing history; and "history," as John Mason opined in his
Brief History of the Pequot War (1736), "most properly is a Declaration of Things that are done by those that were present at the
doing of them."[15] Far from impugning the Americanness of
Oroonoko, Behn's apparent cribbing from Warren and Tryon simply adds one more item to the list of generic conventions—the
almost paranoid anxiety regarding political insurrection,[16] the

digression into promotional puffery, the use of Indian words to describe unfamiliar things, the pointed contrast between natural beauty and human wickedness and suffering, the tendency to order events chronologically rather than thematically, and the employment of a prose style that, associating plainness with honesty, eschews an ornamental display of the writer's status in favor of the direct communication of a perceived world—conventions that, all together, bind her narrative to the earliest and most influential of American literary forms.

Even if Behn really had been to Surinam, that fact would not have required her to say that she had or to present her romantic tale in the form of the Brief True Relation. Indeed, she could have found several excellent reasons for withholding that information. Far from accepting her own unverifiable experience as a basis of authority, many of her readers would have associated such a claim with the confessions of radical dissenters and the memoirs of highwaymen. Not even autobiographers, arguably the most individualistic of seventeenth-century writers, were inclined to rest the rightness of their beliefs on personal experience alone.[17] Only in the narratives of New World travelers do we find the authority of personal experience so much insisted upon, and even here an aggressively defensive tone often betrays the writer's conviction that his words will not be believed. "I would be loath to broach anything which may puzzle thy belief," says William Wood in the introduction to his New England's Prospect (1634), "and so justly draw upon myself that unjust aspersion commonly laid on travellers, of whom many say, 'They may lie by authority, because none can control them;' which proverb had surely his original from the sleepy belief of many a homebred dormouse, who comprehends not either the rarity or possibility of those things he sees not; of whom it may be said as once of Diogenes, that because he circled himself in the circumstance of a tub, he therefore contemned the port and palace of Alexander, which he knew not. So there is many a tub-trained cynic, who because anything stranger than ordinary is too large for the strait hoops of his apprehension, he peremptorily concludes that it is a lie."[18]

The point is that, despite the potential hazards implicit in the Brief True Relation, Behn modeled her narrative upon that form because it enabled her to live in the old world of romance and the new world of her reader at the same time. Even more to the point, by telling her romantic tale in this form she stumbled, however unwillingly, upon a new way of writing fiction—a combination of language, structure, theme, narrative mode, and vision of human history that we now associate with "the novel."[19] In that respect, *Oroonoko* belongs in the first chapter of any history of American fiction, somewhere between Henry Nevile's *Isle of Pines* (1668) and *Robinson Crusoe* (1714). And to say that is to place it at the very source of the English novel—the novel written in English—for, as *Oroonoko* suggests, the peculiar features of that genre have an apparent source in the narrative form through which America made its way into the English language. Certainly, *Oroonoko* warrants this historical preferment more than does, say, the customarily celebrated *Pilgrim's Progress,* a religious romance that points farther backward than forward in the history of fictional forms,[20] and far more than do the first novels written by American citizens, which did not appear until more than a century later, long after the genre had found its proper subjects and its characteristic voice. One of these soi-disant "early" American novels, Royall Tyler's *The Algerine Captive* (1797), ridicules Behn's attempt to pass off a romantic hero as an actual, historical personage. We notice, however, that Tyler's narrator judges *Oroonoko* from the very ground of truth that this work helped to establish (Underhill saw no royal slaves during *his* captivity), that Tyler's work is also a purportedly True Relation, and that his use of this form led him into difficulties very much like those that *Oroonoko* had caused Behn.[21]

Tyler's apparent need to declare his independence from Behn's century-old novel indicates the peculiar inveteracy of this reputedly minor and obviously flawed little book. Why *Oroonoko* has refused to lie down and die along with the rest of Behn's work and nearly every other piece of seventeenth-century English fiction must remain a puzzle until we notice its tendency to resurface at those times and in those places where the idea of America as an "other World," governed by another kind of truth, has figured prominently in human affairs.[22] Translated into French in 1745, *Oroonoko* went through eight editions by 1799, during the years when France was performing its own bloody rendition of the American revolution. In the nineteenth century, when the word "American" had become nearly synonymous with "radical," Behn's novel found favor with Blake, for whom the American and French revolutions signaled the advent of a new but ultimately timeless world order, and with Swinburne, one of the few people on either side of the Atlantic to realize that Whitman presaged a new order for poetry. By the same token, to those who, like Pope, the aging and repentant Dryden, and the watchdogs of Victorian morality, condemned the social and literary effects of anarchic "American" energies, Behn's work as a whole has always seemed "immoral." From the day *Oroonoko* was written, when analogues to the hero's denunciation of slavery could be found only in the works of radical dissenters like George Fox, until the present day, when Behn has been canonized a feminist saint, she has almost invariably been seen as a rebel.

Radicalism, however, is only half of the story. In her prologue to *The Young King,* ostensibly begun during her youth in Surinam, she says that she "fear'd the Reproach of being an American" (2:105), meaning a sort of artless barbarian; and there is no reason to suppose that she was merely being coy. Like most of her educated contemporaries and like every reflective New World voyager, she was torn between her veneration of traditional authorities and the exciting prospect of discovering things that the ancients never knew. In the Renaissance debate between the Ancients and the Moderns, which has close connections with the discovery of the New World,[23] Behn aligned herself among the Moderns, proclaiming the superiority of original invention over slavish observance of the classical "rules." But just as Europe received America initially as part of the classical design of history and came only gradually to regard it as an emblem of progress and historical departure,[24] until Behn discovered otherwise in *Oroo-*

noko, she seems to have seen no necessary conflict between modern innovation and the essential spirit of classicism. Modernism was simply a way of realizing that spirit in the present. If she advocated the liberation of women and the sanctity of unlegalized love, that was because these were the original conditions of life in the Golden Age. If she sought to reinterpret Scripture in the light of Copernican science, that was to rescue the Bible from the superstitions of the Dark Ages and from the rebellious designs of radical dissenters alike. If she introduced "novelties" into her plays and romances, these were carefully constrained within the justifying forms of well-established genres. Despite her early and continuing reputation for radicalism, her rebellions were invariably staged on behalf of conservative, not to say reactionary, principles.

Behn's departure from romance form in *Oroonoko* appears to have been simply one more extravagant maneuver in this reactionary campaign, an attempt to recover the vanished past by pursuing history westward, around the world to its beginning. Until Byam and his men of the new England interfere, the action is headed straight for a marriage of love and honor, of feminine nature and masculine control,[25] in one of those sacramental wedding rites that, concluding the action in romances, symbolize the eternal redemption of human history. What Behn expected to issue from the union of Oroonoko and Imoinda may be seen in the following lines from her *Congratulatory Poem to Her Most Sacred Majesty on the Universal Hopes of All Loyal Persons for a Prince of Wales* (1687):

> Like the first sacred infant, this will come
> With promise laden from the blessed womb,
> To call the wand'ring scatter'd nations home;

and in these, from her *Congratulatory Poem to Her Sacred Majesty Queen Mary, Upon Her Arrival in England* (1689):

> The Murmuring World till now divided lay,
> Vainly debating whom they shou'd Obey,
> Till You Great Caesar's Off-spring blest our Isle
> The differing Multitudes to Reconcile. . . . [26]

The America portrayed in the Brief True Relation, unfortunately, was not a place out of time or at the end of time. It was, rather, a new historical era, whose place in the eternal design could not be known until its continually expanding, shifting form and its elusive significance were finally comprehended. When accumulating human knowledge might arrive at that destination was anybody's guess. The great day, which had seemed to Columbus so close at hand, had already been deferred countless times by 1688, and the ever-receding goal of Old World desire now lay farther ahead than ever before, beyond the chimerical horizon. Transported to this landscape of obscurely destined history, the romantic marriage lost its sacramental relation with the divine scheme of things and became merely another link in the lengthening chain of hopes deferred and expectations revised. When the expedition to America seemed a journey to Eden, marriage might betoken the redemption of all of those conflicting human desires that had prompted the journey. But when those desires, seduced by the historical opportunities they uncovered in the New World, "for empire . . . did *Eden* change; / Less charming . . . and [of] far less worth" (6:144), when the path to Eden turned into the course of empire, then the ancient forms of justification would no longer serve. As Behn discovered to her dismay, voyaging in the "other World" leads, in time, to a new and terrible knowledge: we made that world and are solely responsible for it. After such knowledge, what forgiveness?

Oroonoko, of course, was to find its vindication in history, in all of those later novels of which Behn's little book seems, to our privileged hindsight, a clear foreshadowing. Its thematic conflict of ancient formalities with modern energies; its portrait of the hero as a Royal Slave, a prince enfettered by brute circumstance; its story of children leaving their parents' home to search for a new, more perfect one; its depiction of history as "character development"; its location of reality in the interplay between a perceived world and a perceiving consciousness; its language, which lends poetic eloquence to the most prosaic things by making them the correlative objects of motions in the human soul; its ambiva-

lent attitude of nostalgia for a vanishing world and eager antici-
pation of a coming one; its divided allegiances to its audience and
to its own discovered truths—these are the very stuff of what we
call "the novel," the modern literary form that was devised to deal
with the new world that America made.

For Behn herself, however, the impending history that would
rescue *Oroonoko* from history by making it a novel was a prospect
too awful even to contemplate. Lying on her deathbed in 1689,
less than a year after the publication of *Oroonoko* and the final
deposition of her beloved Stuarts, she responded in verse to an
invitation by one Dr. Burnet to enlist her muse in the service of
the new England. The metaphor by which she excuses herself
from this unwelcome duty associates the headlong rush of current
events, at once, with the ancient book of Exodus and the modern
European migration to America:

> My Muse . . . would endeavour fain to glide
> With the fair prosperous Gale, and the full driving Tide,
> But Loyalty Commands with Pious Force,
> That stops me in the thriving Course,
> The Brieze that wafts the Crowding Nations o'er,
> Leaves me unpity'd far behind
> On the Forsaken Barren Shore,
> To sigh with Echo, and the Murmuring Wind;
> While all the exciting Prospect I survey,
> With Melancholy Eyes I view the Plains,
> Where all I see is Ravishing and Gay,
> And all I hear is Mirth in loudest Strains;
> Thus while the Chosen Seed possess the Promis'd Land,
> I like the Excluded Prophet stand,
> The Fruitful Happy Soil can only see
> But am forbid by Fates Decree
> To share the Triumph of the joyful Victory. (6:409)

Read in the context of Behn's adventures with Oroonoko, this
image of the Excluded Prophet, debarred by ancient loyalties and
the decree of fate from entering the Promised Land, where her

muse would gladly go, has a wonderful irony. For the Promised Land that calls the Crowding Nations across the Atlantic is, as Oroonoko discovered, an Old World dream, already dispelled by the efforts to realize it; while the dishonored prophet, who seems to sit on the Forsaken Barren Shore of the Old World, consoling herself with the devalued bric-a-brac of antique legend, has in fact been there ahead of the rest and has already learned what it will take the Chosen Seed another two hundred years to realize—that the old world is gone and that the new one will require its makers to conceive an entirely new idea of their collective destiny.

Three Blind Men and an Elephant: The Problem of Nineteenth-Century English

Thus we are driven back upon periods. All divisions falsify our material to some extent; the best one can hope is to choose those which falsify it least.

C. S. LEWIS[1]

The vocabulary of English literary study has a catch phrase for all of the major periods but one. The centuries before 1500 are "the Middle Ages." The sixteenth and seventeenth centuries are "the Renaissance." We call the eighteenth century "Neoclassical" and the twentieth century "Modern." But for the nineteenth century—the first of our literary ages to devise a theory of literary ages, the first to think of itself as an age, and the first to employ the phrase "spirit of the age"—we have no name.

Instead, we have names for parts of the period—Romantic, Victorian, and American—presumably because the subject, unlike the Middle Ages and the Renaissance, is too large, too complex to be taken in at a glance. If that were really the case, some sort of piecemeal approach would be quite in order. By dividing this unwieldy period into manageable segments we could come to an understanding of the whole. The actual case, however, appears to be that our inability to comprehend the whole is as much a result of our present subdivisions as a justification for them. Although Romantic, Victorian, and American literature are subcategories of nineteenth-century English, they cannot possibly be reassembled to give us a coherent picture of that subject because they have been formed on basically different logical principles. Romantic literature is writing on a certain *kind*. Victorian literature is the work of a particular *time*. And American literature comes from a

77

certain *place*. As a result, neither are the three subcategories logically compatible, establishing some necessary relation among Romantic, Victorian, and American works, nor are they mutually exclusive, precluding the existence, say, of a Romantic work written in America during the Victorian period.

This confused situation has prompted some rather frantic efforts to make the three subcategories both more compatible and more distinct. Whereas the term "Romantic" was invented to describe a certain kind of writing, we often attach it to the time when that kind of writing emerged, the Romantic era, which lies next to, but is supposedly different from, the Victorian period. Conversely, although "Victorian" was originally the name of a period, the term has come to denote certain literary traits that are thought to be both characteristic of the period and distinguishable from Romantic ones. And "American," in current literary parlance, refers less often to all works written in that place than to certain works from that place whose subjects or techniques purportedly distinguish them from British works of the same period.

But these attempts to put Humpty-Dumpty together again only make the problem worse. Once we think of romanticism as belonging to a certain period—from 1798 to 1832, say—we are forced to explain why, having once got under way, this supposedly new and significant literary movement stopped so abruptly. The idea of a Romantic era, moreover, suggests that Romantic works were statistically normal in the period, whereas only a small portion of the writing published in those years can be considered Romantic in any sense. Or at least it implies that all of the really important works of the time were Romantic, whereas the period includes Gibbon's *Decline and Fall of the Roman Empire* and the novels of Jane Austen. The idea also implies that Romantic works were not written outside the period, leaving us no way to account for "The Scholar Gypsy" or "The Garden of Proserpine"—to say nothing, for the moment, of *Nature, Walden, Mardi,* and *Leaves of Grass*. By the same token, when we use the word "Victorian" to designate certain literary traits, we unavoidably suggest that some works written in the Victorian period are not Victorian and that some written earlier or later may be Victorian nonetheless. And when we reserve the term "American" for works of a particular sort written in that place, we necessarily exclude a great deal of what was in fact produced there, even as we suggest that the works selected are representative of American writing as a whole.

If these subcategories really were created to help us take hold of English literature in the nineteenth century, they seem particularly ill-suited to the task. Indeed, they obscure important literary facts that are otherwise quite plain. To think of Emerson as a representative American is to associate him more closely with Irving and Cooper, whose works resemble his about as much as do those of Southey and Scott, than with Coleridge and Carlyle, who were his acknowledged teachers, or with Arnold, who considered him the most important English prose writer of the age. By calling "The Rime of the Ancient Mariner" a "Romantic" poem we confer greater importance on its accidental similarities to Keats's odes than on its American sources and theme or its piously prescriptive, "Victorian" moral. And when we label *News from Nowhere* "Victorian," we detach it from *Ivanhoe*, which shares its affection for the Middle Ages, and from *Looking Backward*, which concurs in its utopian socialism, and connect it with Macaulay's *History of England*, which is hostile to both of these outré sentiments.

Because these terms were devised by writers of the period to remove themselves from the shadow of their immediate predecessors and contemporaries, they tend to overemphasize distinctions among things that are in fact quite closely related. The Romantics rebelled against neoclassicism, but Keats studied Dryden. The Victorians claimed to have outgrown romanticism, but Tennyson imitated Keats. The Americans declared their literary independence from Britain, but Poe considered Tennyson the poet of poets. And no Briton ever read an American book, but Rossetti borrowed from Poe. In place of these actual connections, the terms posit vague or excessively recondite conceptual relations among those writers they throw into involuntary association—

"Romantics" like Byron and Lamb, for example, or "Victorians" like Arnold and Swinburne, or "Americans" like Whittier and Whitman. Seldom are the shared traits that permit such groupings the ones by which we identify any individual member of the group. What are we to understand the word "Romantic" to mean if it includes both *Prometheus Unbound* and "The Ruined Cottage," or "Victorian" if it describes *The Old Curiosity Shop* and Swinburne's "The Leper," or "American" when it embraces *The Mysterious Stranger* and *The Rise of Silas Lapham*?

The logic and utility of these terms have not gone unquestioned, by any means. Over fifty years ago, A. O. Lovejoy observed that "the word 'romantic' has come to mean so many things that, by itself, it means nothing. It has ceased to perform the function of a verbal sign."[2] The controversy stirred by Lovejoy's essay remains unresolved as far as romanticism is concerned and has spilled over into the adjacent Victorian period, raising explicit questions about the proper use of that term and generating a number of major studies that simply ignore the customary boundaries between the Romantic, Victorian, and Modern periods in order to trace an unbroken movement from romanticism to modernism.[3] Insofar as these attempts to discover some coherence in the nineteenth century have blurred the line between Romantic and Modern writing, they have met resistance from critics who advocate a distinct Romantic period.[4] And insofar as they have dropped the term "Victorian," they have occasioned some efforts to reinstate that category in its intermediary position.[5] Nevertheless, the clear tendency of recent nineteenth-century studies is to take a more comprehensive view of the subject than the terms Romantic and Victorian allow, even if that requires calling the whole period Romantic.[6]

On the question of excluding American works from the subject, matters have not gone nearly so far. Still, there are signs of increasing disgruntlement with the provinciality of American literature as that subject is presently constituted and of a growing interest in the literary relations between America and England in the nine-

teenth century. In "What Is American Literature?" I argue that
while this category logically includes every work, in every language, having to do with the New World as a whole since the
discovery, in actual practice the term designates a mere handful of
works written in English, in the United States, mainly in the nineteenth century.[7] This de facto definition makes the subject part
of English literature—of literature in English—and therefore
obliges us to study it in that context rather than separately. To be
sure, many studies have compared British and American writings
from the nineteenth century. But these have normally aimed to
identify differences (often very dubious ones) between the two
national literatures and thus to justify, rather than to question,
their separate treatment. Still, one can find in recent criticism instances of a less prejudicial attitude toward British-American literary relations: a growing number of studies that simply ignore
the national origin of the works treated and one or two that consider the impact of British and American writings on each other.[8]
The signs of restiveness are as yet faint, but they point to a reconsideration of "American" literature very much like those to which
the terms "Romantic" and "Victorian" are now being subjected.

   On a more general level, John M. Ellis has recently enumerated
the logical and practical problems that attend the use of all such
"primitive" terms in theoretical discourse.[9] Words like "romantic"
and "realistic," Ellis contends, originate in common parlance,
where they serve, usefully, to communicate rather vague but generally understood bundles of more or less related ideas. We know
what such terms mean until we try to define them. Once they are
taken out of everyday speech and put to theoretical use, however,
they must be defined, and so we set out to clarify the vague meanings they were originally designed to convey. These attempts at
definition usually take the form of assertions that some term does
not mean what we have always thought but something quite different. Propositions of this sort, in turn, provoke rejoinders: the
term doesn't mean that at all but something else again. There thus
arises an extended controversy regarding the "real" meaning of

the word. Each new definition seeks to cancel out all previous definitions but succeeds only in adding one more item to the list, thereby complicating the very problem it aimed to solve.

With so many definitions to choose from, anyone who writes on the subject to which the term refers must either use the term naively, as if its meaning were generally understood, or define it once again in the vain hope of settling the question once and for all, or simply stipulate the meaning that the term will bear in this particular instance. But no matter which of these alternatives the writer chooses, the disagreement will remain. Every proposition that uses the term will be a definition of the term, and the literary works about which the proposition is made will become evidence in support of that definition. In short, the proposition will be a tautology. If we say that Romantic poetry seeks to heal the Cartesian split between subject and object, we are not proposing something about an established category of poems, we are defining the category: Romantic poems are those that seek to heal this division. And since the poems we select to support this pseudo-proposition will obviously fit the definition, the proposition cannot be disproved. Or rather, it can be disproved only by a counterproposition that will define the category differently in order to admit different poems into evidence. Little wonder that studies of Romantic, Victorian, and American literature so often degenerate into squabbles over the meaning of these terms, with the literature itself, which is ostensibly our main concern, relegated to service on behalf of the various arguments being advanced.

Given this situation, the only logically defensible study of Romantic, Victorian, and American literature would be a history of the various ways in which these terms have been used and an explanation of why they have been used in these ways at different times.[10] Since our present subject is English literature of the nineteenth century, rather than the meaning of these terms, and since they seem to impede rather than to assist our understanding of that subject, I propose that we drop them, not with any confident expectation that they will in fact go out of use but merely to see for a moment what the subject looks like without them. What immediately appears when these incompatible subdivisions are removed is a category whose definition—unlike that of Romantic, Victorian, and American literature—does not depend upon some prior interpretation of its contents. Until someone comes up with a catchier title, we can call this subject simply nineteenth-century English literature—which is to say, literature (however narrowly or broadly one chooses to define *that* difficult term) written in English between the end of the eighteenth century and the beginning of the twentieth.

The only thing this definition needs to make it complete and usable is a more precise historical demarcation, preferably of the sort employed to delimit the other periods of English literature.[11] "Medieval" and "Renaissance," for example, (although not without their own border disputes) denote literary periods bounded by cataclysmic nonliterary events. The Middle Ages extend from the date of the earliest known English texts to the invention of printing or the discovery of the New World or the Protestant Reformation; while the Renaissance extends to the Stuart Restoration. This system of periodization breaks down, we note, as we approach the nineteenth century. The end of the period that we call "the Restoration and eighteenth century" moves around with our changing interpretations of "romanticism," "the Romantic era," and the "pre-Romantics"; and from that point on, the historical model fails to apply.

By getting rid of the term "Romantic," however, we can resurrect the model. Our period might then begin with the great revolutions in France and British America, events that are at once comparable in magnitude to those by which we demarcate the Middle Ages and the Renaissance and a good deal more significant of the general literary situation at the end of the eighteenth century than is any single literary event—the publication of *Lyrical Ballads,* for instance.[12] The American and French revolutions were the culmination of Enlightenment thought. They signaled to people of the

time the dawning of a new age, welcome or not, and they set in
motion the forces of social, political, and intellectual change that
perplexed and excited the entire nineteenth century. Equally important for our purposes, they mark the beginning of the period
in which the recognized classics of "American literature" were
written (all earlier American writings in English being normally
considered foreshadowings of these national masterpieces),
thereby conjoining the starting point of our complete subject,
nineteenth-century literature in English, with that of its American
component.

Attempts to date the close of our literary period have been bedeviled by the same problem we found at its beginning: just as
"romanticism" seems to have no clear starting point, "Victorian"
writing does not seem to stop with Victoria's death but to linger
on through the "Edwardian" and "Georgian" periods, long after
"modernism" has emerged from its obscure origins. By dropping
the term "Victorian," however, we can avoid the dispute about
where the "Victorian temper" gives way to the "Modern spirit"
and set our boundary line at World War I, another nonliterary
event of nonetheless enormous literary significance.[13] Like the
revolutions that climaxed the Enlightenment, the Great War
seemed to those who lived through it the logical conclusion to
what had gone before and the beginning of an altogether new
condition of life. To us, the war seems no less cataclysmic, opening
an abyss between our world and one that, although deceptively
near to us in time, we can understand only with a conscious effort
of the historical imagination—a time, for example, when "going
to heaven" could be used without irony as a poetic metaphor.
Then too, as the eighteenth-century revolutions mark the point
where the curriculum of English literature separates into British
and American courses, World War I marks the point where these
streams reunite to form the single course we call the twentieth
century, in which the literary works of Britain and America are
studied more often together, as instances of international modernism, than separately, as products of their respective national cultures.[14]

Disputable as these particular boundaries may be, the definition of our subject as literature written in English between 1775 and 1918 has several clear advantages over our customary tripartite scheme. First of all, it includes and gives equal value, at least initially, to every literary work written in English in the period, instead of conferring preeminence on those works that happen to support our notions concerning the nature of Romantic, Victorian and American writing. We can therefore proceed, as students of medieval or Renaissance literature presumably do, from a general agreement about what the subject contains to an inquiry into the character, meaning, and value of those contents, instead of getting bogged down, as we now tend to do, in unresolvable debates over the definitions of our categories and what they properly contain. Second, the period as defined is sufficiently large in itself and sufficiently distinct from those that precede and follow it to have a character of its own, whatever that character may turn out to be when its contents have all been inspected. At the same time, because the period is formed on the same principles as are its neighboring periods, it can be related to them. Whereas recent attempts to trace the Romantic movement through the Victorian period or to trace modernism back to the Romantic era have had to struggle against entrenched attitudes regarding the dates of those subdivisions, there is nothing in the definition of nineteenth-century English literature to prevent our tracing whatever we find there back into the eighteenth century or ahead to the twentieth. What is more, because English literature from 1775 to 1918 is defined on linguistic and historical principles that pertain throughout the Western world, it can be compared with contemporaneous literatures in other languages, something that is not possible when the subject is broken up into parts that have no exact counterparts elsewhere.[15]

But the main virtue of this comprehensive definition, to my mind, is the freedom and encouragement it gives us to stop quarreling over what Romantic, Victorian, and American "really" mean and to think instead about the larger question that these subcategories were presumably created to help us answer: What is the nature—the shape and direction—of nineteenth-century English literature as a whole? It is a difficult question, to be sure; our inability to give the period a name demonstrates that fact. At the same time, the question is perhaps less difficult now than it was when these subcategories were first devised, simply because, knowing what came later, we know where the nineteenth- century is heading, so to speak, and can identify more precisely the tendencies that got it there. To illustrate the possibility of considering nineteenth-century English literature as a single subject and what seem to me the advantages of doing so, I want to suggest one way that the subject might be organized. I make no claims for the originality of this scheme. On the contrary, its terms are quite familiar. I offer it only to indicate the sort of comprehensive treatment I think the subject needs and to suggest that the overall shape of the period may not be as difficult to grasp as our present system of subdivisions implies—that these subdivisions may themselves be responsible for our feeling that the period is unmanageable.

II

When nineteenth-century English literature is viewed conspectively, as a single literary development, rather than as a mixed bag of intellectual, social, and national movements, there can be seen to run throughout it, from beginning to end, a debate between two distinct but closely related ideas concerning the fundamental nature of reality. On one side is the idea that reality is grounded in eternally ordained *forms* that precede, govern, and give meaning to all human and natural actions. On the other side is the idea that reality arises from formless *energy*: the motive power behind the temporal events that constitute human and natural history.[16] While it is possible to characterize many writers of the period as tending toward one or the other of these two positions, the debate is more a contest of ideas than of persons. The point at issue is not the existence of motivating energy or of significant forms, both of which are acknowledged to be necessary elements of reality, but

the priority and the relative value of these two entities in the determination of reality. Which came first: the meaning of events or
the events themselves? Which is the substance of reality and which
is its shadow? And this fundamental question can assume any
number of guises. What determines knowledge: the mental forms
into which experience is poured or the frame of mind that a particular course of thoughts and experiences happens to produce?
How is human behavior to be judged: against unchanging principles of right and wrong or in the light of moral conditions arising out of the behavior itself? What is the basis of political authority: inherited tradition or the aspirations of the governed? What
is the measure of aesthetic value: the ingenious demonstration of
existing ideas about the good, the true, and the beautiful or the
radical redefinition of these ideas through symbolic actions?

These questions concerning the ontological, epistemological,
ethical, political, and aesthetic priority of form and energy are not
in themselves peculiar to the nineteenth century, of course. The
sources of the debate are ancient, and its history can be traced
through the Middle Ages, the Renaissance, and the eighteenth
century. In the nineteenth century, however, the debate became
especially urgent, a matter of unprecedented concern, owing
partly to the steady erosion throughout the Enlightenment of received beliefs concerning the eternal structure of reality and partly
to the accelerating pace of social, economic, political, and intellectual change in the nineteenth century itself. And it is this felt urgency that distinguishes the nineteenth century both from earlier
periods, in which the debate is present but not yet either so mo-
mentous or so widely acknowledged, and from the twentieth century, in which the debate, although still detectable, has become far
less urgent, largely because of what happened in the nineteenth
century.[17]

What happened in those years between 1775 and 1918 may be
described as a more or less steady shift, traceable in literary works
of acknowledged importance, from the formal to the energetic
side of the debate: a gradual abandonment of the belief that ac-

tions arise from and fulfill some absolute, unchanging form and a gradual acceptance of the idea that actions—whether historical, natural, or literary—generate the forms that give them meaning. While most of the writing published throughout the period remains loyal to the traditional view of history as the enaction of a timeless design, the literary mainstream can be seen to diverge increasingly from this official view toward the idea that forms are only the products—whether necessary, accidental, or artificial—of human action. At the beginning of the period, the principle of form is largely in command. While literary opinion on the value of energetic action is sharply divided between fear of its danger to existing religious, social, and political institutions and faith in its ability to recover or to discover absolute truths, even the most enthusiastic celebrations of unfettered energy tend to rest their case, ultimately, upon the pertinence of such actions to some absolute form. By the end of the period, however, the center of literary opinion has shifted markedly. Although a number of literarily important writings continue to support the faith of the official culture and the general reader in the primacy of eternal forms, the prevailing view among writers of genius is that all forms are contingent upon the apparently undirected course of temporal events. A conspectus of the period, then, reveals, first, an uninterrupted dialogue on a single pressing question: the relation between form and action; second, a steady growth, beginning at about the time of the American Revolution, in the authority and influence of the energetic side of this debate; and third, a concurrent diminution in the volume and range of the formal voice, culminating in the din of World War I.

To illustrate this development we can think, first, of Benjamin Franklin's *Autobiography* and Blake's *The Marriage of Heaven and Hell* as representative of the literary situation at the end of the eighteenth century. Although these two works seem utterly opposed, with Franklin preaching the submission of impulsive action to the rule of Universal Reason and Blake demanding the liberation of creative human energy from all such "mind-forged manacles," they are united in their determination to justify creative individual actions in the name of some enduring form of the truth. By the middle of the nineteenth century, energies of the sort that Franklin wished to control and that Blake wanted to see unleashed have outstripped the ability of traditional forms to comprehend them, leaving Tennyson to wonder whether the runaway forces of modern life can ever be squared with inherited systems of belief and Melville to ponder the darkly ambiguous consequences of unconstrained creative action. And when we come to the end of our period, we find the principle of energy in almost total literary command. While popular romancers and versifiers dream of recovering the lost ground of ancient forms in the past or in the future, in as yet undamaged sections of the countryside, in the domestic circle or the church, Henry James is looking for some way to derive value and meaning from human action alone, and T. S. Eliot is trying to find some motive for action in the absence of all signifying, validating forms.

To be sure, the merits of this particular scheme and the placement of individual works within it can be disputed endlessly. Nevertheless, a comprehensive model of this sort seems to me vastly superior to our customary division of the period into Romantic, Victorian, and American compartments. Unlike the ostensibly unique traits by which those categories are said to be identified and distinguished from each other, the debate between form and energy shows up everywhere: at every stage of the period, in every place where literature is written in English, and in every major literary work written in these various times and places. It may appear as a basic temperamental difference between writers publishing at about the same time, like Ann Radcliffe and Charles Brockden Brown, or Dickens and Carlyle, or Arnold Bennett and Virginia Woolf. It may appear as an inconsistency among different works composed by the same writer at different times: like Scott's *Waverley* and *Ivanhoe,* for example, or Tennyson's *Idylls of the King* and "Ulysses," or Mark Twain's *Joan of Arc* and *Roughing It.* Or it may appear in the ideological and structural distinctions between works written by different writers at different times—between *Pride and Prejudice* and *Sister Carrie,* say, or Masefield's "The Everlasting Mercy" and Freneau's "The House of Night." But it is within individual works that the debate shows up most clearly and significantly, and there are few, if any, major works of the period that cannot be described usefully in its terms.

The contesting principles of form and energy assume various metaphorical guises in these works, ranging from the most discursively abstract to the most symbolically concrete. Sometimes they appear as naked ideas: Emerson's metaphysical concepts of form and power, the final "position" of Newman's mind and the "history of opinions" that led up to it, and Coleridge's literary distinction between the moral destination of a work and the poetic journey by which we arrive there. Often the debate takes the more concrete shape of a conflict between characters: Keats's Apollonius and Lamia, Dickens's Floy and Dombey, Cooper's Hetty and Judith. It may appear as a divided setting, whether the division is spatial—the town and the forest of "Goblin Market," country and city in "Tintern Abbey," the farmhouse and the woods in *A Boy's Will*—or temporal—Scott's present and past, Carlyle's past and present, Bellamy's future and present. And sometimes the two principles appear as pure thematic symbols: Blake's cistern and fountain, Arnold's culture and anarchy, Dreiser's rocking chair and train.

The debate may operate on several levels at once, as in Tennyson's *In Memoriam,* where the contest is simultaneously stylistic, pitting the rhetoric of communal belief against the effusions of personal sorrow; thematic, contrasting the authority of received doctrine with that of experienced grief; structural, setting the principle of intentionally imposed form against that of fortuitously achieved form; and symbolic, opposing Phosphor to Hesper. Indeed, the critical reputation of most nineteenth-century works is generally proportional to the breadth and subtlety of their treatment of this ubiquitous question. While almost no work of the period can be said to ignore the problem, and although every work that takes it up is bound to acknowledge both of its constituent terms, those works that seem to us minor tend to argue the exclusive truth of one side and the utter falsity of the other; whereas those we regard as masterpieces seek to adjudicate the conflict between these mutually exclusive but equally authoritative ideas. For Blake, salvation lies neither in the anarchic energies of Orc nor in the repressive forms of Urizen but in the creative powers of Los, which are bound by their own liberating forms. *The Scarlet Letter* advocates neither Hester's passionate energies nor Dimmesdale's spiritual laws but rather their perfect union in Pearl, who is the oneness of their divided being. Because intellectual calm and emotional vitality are, for Wordsworth, "the sister horns of nature," neither can be denied, and *The Prelude* must find a way to resolve the conflict between them—if not in some final form that has a "law," a "meaning," and an "end," then in those timeless "spots of time" where the eternal "frame of things" and the onward motions of the soul achieve momentary equipoise. As "Mont Blanc" is both the Law and the Power, and as opium brings De Quincey "infinite repose" amid "infinite activity," the seasons in *Walden* denote both the passing of time and the eternal return of spring. No matter how variously these masterworks define the solution—whether as a moral understanding, as a transcendent vision, or as a symbolic ambiguity—they are drawn together by the enduring question of the age and exalted by their artistic comprehension of its endless ramifications.

Because this debate manifests itself everywhere in the period, it enables us to acknowledge and explain many facts that our present subcategories seem to regard as embarrassments. Instead of dividing the prominent writers of the 1780s and 1790s into eighteenth-century and Romantic camps, it permits us to see Sheridan and Blake, Fanny Burney and "Monk" Lewis, Gibbon and Burns as participants in a single evolving dialogue on a topic of common concern. Once we stop thinking of 1815 as a year in the Romantic era, we can deal with the fact that *Frankenstein* and *Northanger Abbey* were both published on that date. When we look for instances of this debate, rather than of romanticism or Victorianism, we accept the propinquity of *Suspiria de Profundis* and *Vanity Fair* instead of begging the question with such terms as "Victorian romanticism." And by applying the model throughout the English-speaking world, we can avoid such mare's-nest questions as whether Longfellow or Melville represents the true spirit of American literature—a choice that has forced us to ignore one and then the other of these important writers in the past fifty years—and regard them as equally representative of Anglo-America's peculiar interest in the great debate of the nineteenth century.

Among the lines of relation that remain hidden by our present system of subdivisions but become visible when we think of nineteenth-century English literature as being engaged in a debate on the relative values of form and energy, the connection between British and American writings seem to me in many respects to be the most striking. The thematic and structural emphasis given to the idea that human action creates the forms from which those acts derive their meaning and value—in works like *The Marriage of Heaven and Hell,* "The Ancient Mariner," *Waverley,* and *Sartor Resartus* (all of which associate disruptive, creative energy with America)—owes a great deal to the deep interest of their authors in the American adventure, especially as portrayed in the narratives of New World explorers, settlers, and travelers. Conversely, the extensive development of this idea in American works like "The Raven," "Roger Malvin's Burial," *Pierre,* and *Huckleberry Finn* owes just as much to literary techniques their authors learned from Coleridge, Keats, Carlyle, and De Quincey. Although these American works often seem to us the most important because they foreshadow the concerns and techniques of literary modernism, our model reminds us that in their own time they were overshadowed by the work of writers like Longfellow, Whittier, Lowell, and Harriet Beecher Stowe, who held the more traditional view that every human action manifests as eternal, universal design and whose literary methods of demonstrating the shape of this design were borrowed in large part from Wordsworth, Tennyson, Arnold, and Dickens. What our model suggests, in sum, is that much of what has been called "Romantic" in British literature springs initially from American sources, that much of what has been called "American" is an extension of one important strain of "romanticism" into the Victorian era, and that much of what has been called "Victorian" is better understood as a weakening resistance, in America as well as in England, to a heterodox idea that erupted late in the eighteenth century and developed throughout the nineteenth into the twentieth-century program we call modernism.[18]

In illuminating such relations among conventionally dissociated things within the nineteenth century, it seems, this comprehensive model also reveals connections between the nineteenth century and its flanking periods. Insofar as the formal position, descending from the rationalization of medieval Christianity in the Enlightenment, represents the widespread adoption of previously advanced and unpopular ideas, while the energetic position evolves into the official program of modernism, the apparent shift from formal to energetic dominance over the course of the nineteenth century lines out a path between eighteenth- and twentieth-century writing that is obscured by the customary interposition of the Victorian era between Blake, Coleridge, and Poe on the one hand and Yeats, Eliot, and Stevens on the other. Once these obstacles are removed, we can see the Modernist movement as a direct outgrowth of nineteenth-century literary history, rather than as a radical departure from it, with the adversary culture of the nineteenth century becoming the dominant literary culture— to some extent, even the popular culture—of the twentieth, very much as the elite culture of the eighteenth century became the official culture of the nineteenth.[19] Once we make this connection, moreover, we can perhaps understand what the Modernists meant by "the nineteenth century" when they professed to be reacting against it, instead of merely taking them at their word.

Indeed, the number of potentially interesting questions raised by this model seems to me almost limitless. If we associate energy with poetry, and form with prose, as nineteenth-century writers on both sides of the debate appear to have done, we may ask why there are no British counterparts, until very late in the century, to the short fiction of Irving, Hawthorne, Poe, and Melville.[20] Conversely, why are there so few American counterparts, until equally late in the century, to the narrative poems of Coleridge, Keats, and Byron? And how do we account for the striking similarities between these American stories and British poems—between "Ligeia" and "Christabel," say, or "Rappaccini's Daughter" and "The Eve of St. Agnes"?[21] Why do so many of the narrative poems that Americans did write during the century—"Evangeline," "The Courtship of Miles Standish," "The Vision of Sir Launfal," and "Snow-Bound," for example—seem, for all of their putative "romanticism," to be modeled on the British novel of domestic sentiment and to resemble versifications of the genre by Tennyson and Arnold; while the British equivalents of such American novels as *Arthur Gordon Pym* and *Moby-Dick* must be sought outside fiction in the poems of Coleridge or the "impassioned prose" of De Quincey?

Continuing this line of inquiry, what can the increasing association, during the nineteenth century, of the word "poetic" with the principle of energy, and of the word "prosaic" with the principle of form, tell us about Arnold's turn from poetry to prose and about the contrary movements of Melville and Hardy? What does this same association of ideas tell us about Virginia Woolf's distinction between the prosaic Edwardians and poetic Georgians?[22] What does her formulation, in turn, owe to Hardy, whose novels are rooted more deeply in the poetry of Wordsworth and Coleridge than they are in the novels of Jane Austen or Thackeray, and to Henry James, whose debts to the notoriously unprosaic fiction of Hawthorne are well known? To what extent does Richard Chase's still widely accepted dictum, that "the American novel is a romance" (by which he means "poetic"), rest on D. H. Lawrence's prior application of Woolf's formula to "classic" (again read "poetic") American literature as a whole, fiction and poetry alike,[23] thus closing a transatlantic circuit of influence that runs from Hawthorne to James to Woolf to Lawrence and back, via Chase, to James and Hawthorne? And finally, what does this transference of the word "poetic" from conventional verse forms to fictions built on symbolic action—a transference that begins with Blake, Coleridge, and Emerson and culminates in James and Yeats—tell us about Pound's opinion that poetry should be at least as well written as prose?

III

Once again, I am not arguing for the adoption of this particular scheme. I have outlined it only to suggest the possibilities for research and critical speculation that can arise when nineteenth-century English literature is studied as one subject rather than three. Nor is this to say that the literary traits we now call Romantic or Victorian or American do not exist. Blake, Tennyson, and Emily Dickinson are obviously very different writers, as our present terminology suggests. The point is that the traits usually designated by these terms do not exist solely in works of the type, period, or place to which the terms refer. Blake is not more different from Tennyson and Dickinson than he is from Byron, and he does not resemble Wordsworth nearly as much as he does Hawthorne or Yeats. Nor does the construction of a comprehensive model like the one I have proposed require us to ignore the differences that our present subcategories were created to recognize. Shelley, Wilde, and Melville were all rebels against what I have called the official culture of the nineteenth century, but their rebellions took very different forms as a result of the times and places in which they worked. Jane Austen, Arnold, and Longfellow, by the same token, were all defenders of the traditional verities that were under attack in the period, but their conservative efforts differ because they arose from very different circumstances. Such differences determine the overall shape of the subject, and whatever model we devise for the period will have value only insofar as it can accommodate complexities that our present tripartite system must ignore.

My proposal is not meant to proscribe any topic or method of study whatsoever. There is nothing in the idea of nineteenth-century English literature as a single subject to prevent someone from studying the literary effects of Wordsworth's relations with the Lake Poets, of Tennyson's appointment as Victoria's poet laureate, or of Melville's attempts to write a novel in English that would yet be non-British. On the contrary, my aim is to remove from the subject those dubious categories that now seem either to discourage such investigations or to prejudice their conclusions. The general drift of English literature in the nineteenth century is determined by the actions of those who wrote it, not by the categories we have imposed upon it; and we can chart that drift only by attending very closely to such specific matters.

I am arguing against the overspecialization, the provincialism, the inflation of decidedly minor talents and the fragmented learning that attend the compartmentalization of nineteenth-century English into Romantic, and Victorian, and American studies. We spend so much time studying and teaching the differences among Romantic, Victorian, and American writing that neither we nor our students are ever encouraged to consider the great revolutionary movement in literary thought and technique to which these various writings all contributed. There are too many students of romanticism who have never read Emerson or Melville, too many students of Victorian literature who know nothing of Wordsworth and Keats, too many majors in American literature who think that Puritanism influenced only American writing. But what more can we expect of these students, when professors of American literature have never seriously asked whether American writing in English really has a character and a history of its own, and professors of British literature seek to ingratiate themselves with the ghost of Sydney Smith by sneering at American books? When graduate students can't quite decide whether Jane Austen, not being a Romantic, is a holdover from the eighteenth century or a precocious Victorian, can't identify Swinburne's kinship with Shelley and Whitman, and think that Mark Twain sprang unsired from the American soil, then something is obviously wrong, something that a basic course in nineteenth-century English literature would help to repair.

Scholars in fields other than English are, of course, perfectly free to go on using nineteenth-century English writings in whatever ways seem useful to them. Romanticism appears to be a more workable concept in French and German literature than it is in English, and there is no reason why comparatists should not consider under that rubric any English work that fits it. A historian of British society in Victoria's reign is not obligated to read *Hard Times* in relation to *Songs of Experience* and "Bartleby the Scrivener." And in a field like American Studies, where the bias remains more historical and sociological than literary, there may be some justification for treating *Song of Myself* as an American event, apart from Blake's *America* and Mill's *On Liberty*. But if English literature is really our subject—if, indeed, it is to survive as a subject— then we must define it in its own linguistic and literary terms, not in terms that are borrowed from subjects other than literature or from literatures other than English. While it is true that nothing of much importance will be said about English literature by anyone who is ignorant of these subjects or who neglects the information they can provide, neither will we learn anything about English literature in the nineteenth century if we confuse it with German metaphysics or liberal reform in Britain or North American civilization. The literary traits we call Romantic, Victorian, and American, thereby placing them in isolated categories, appear throughout nineteenth-century English literature, albeit in varying degrees, guises, and combinations; and it is through these variations that we can trace the course of English literature from the eighteenth century to the twentieth.

Henry James's The American

Ever since *The American* first appeared in print, over a hundred years ago, readers have been trying to decide what, if anything, is American about the novel. It has been said, more than once, that simply by calling his book *The American* James committed a definitively American act—that no Frenchman, for example, would think of writing a novel called *Le Français*. James himself seems to have lent some credence to this notion when he said, "It is hard to imagine two or three Englishmen, two or three Frenchmen, two or three Germans comparing notes and strongly differing as to the impression made upon the civilized world by the collective body of their countrymen. . . . We are the only people with whom such a question can be in the least what the French call an actuality." Perhaps so. But it is equally hard to imagine an American writing a play about a Frenchman and calling it *The Foreigner*, whereas it was the younger Dumas's unflattering portrait of the American heroine in a melodrama called *L'Étrangère* that provoked James's treatment of Christopher Newman. Nor is Dumas the only European ever to have essayed a definition of the American character. On the contrary, the genre was invented by *étrangers*—Crèvecoeur, Tocqueville, Santayana. And as for those knots of Englishmen, Frenchmen, and Germans who are so indifferent to their own collective impact on the civilized world: have they ever tired of measuring the impression that Americans have made upon civilization? The American has never been an exclusively American subject, neither in Columbus's day nor, certainly, in ours.

James's novel is clearly American in the most common sense of that term, having been written by an American. When applied to literature, however, the word "American" has always denoted something more than nationality of authorship. At least, categorical statements of the sort that American literature seems to invite—that it is democratic or idealistic or realistic or romantic or whatever—cannot possibly include every book ever written by an American. In fact, such statements normally apply only to a very small and select group of American writings—works like *Huckle-berry Finn* and *Leaves of Grass*, whose eccentricities of language and form seem to distinguish them from European, and especially from English, writings. *The American*, however, is notably deficient in these stylistic and structural symptoms of literary Americanness. With nothing but this novel to go on, the reader would have no way of knowing that James was not an Englishman. For that matter, even the nationality of its author can be called into question, since the "American" who wrote it was raised in what he himself called the old "English" America, had already spent a good deal of his life abroad, and had just moved to Europe, where he would spend the rest of his life, eventually renouncing his American citizenship to become a British subject.

Perhaps the Americanness of *The American* resides in its argument: the moral triumph of American good nature over European treachery. To be sure, that was James's original idea for the novel, as he remembered it some thirty years later. "I found myself," James recalled, "considering . . . the situation, in another country and an aristocratic society, of some robust but insidiously beguiled and betrayed, some cruelly wronged, compatriot: the point being in especial that he should suffer at the hands of persons pretending to represent the highest possible civilization and to be of an order in every way superior to his own. What would he 'do' in that predicament? . . . He would hold his revenge and cherish it and feel its sweetness, and then in the very act of forcing it home would sacrifice it in disgust, . . . and he would obey, in doing so, one of the large and easy impulses *generally* characteristic of his type." The idea does seem altogether American, an evocation of America's perennial love-hate relation with Europe and all of its attendant feelings of cultural inferiority and moral superiority, or parricidal guilt and newborn innocence, of nostalgia for the old home and the urge to destroy it.

The question cannot be answered quite so easily, however. James may have set out to celebrate "the large and easy impulses" that are "*generally* characteristic" of Americans, but the characters and the action he devised to express this idea have led many of his readers to wonder whether Newman's type, far from being celebrated in the novel, is not in fact satirized or even morally condemned. Certainly, there is something a little foolish in Newman's social gaucherie, his sublime and largely ungrounded self-confidence; something ill-natured in his inability to sympathize with Claire's feelings of familial obligation; and something downright vicious in his influence upon the lives of Noémie and Valentin. James's attitudes toward his characters are by no means easy to sort out. As a sturdy republican who yet admired the European way of ordering society, who resented the steep condescensions of pretentiously superior Europeans and yet lamented the commercial vulgarization of his "sweet old Anglo-Saxon" America, James found his sympathies sharply divided between the sustaining traditions of the Old World and the unfettered dynamism of the New. From an American point of view, Newman's assumption that he is at the very least the Bellegardes' equal seems perfectly justified. But when the Bellegardes reject him, they do so on ancient, anticommercial principles of the very sort that James missed in America and hoped to recover by moving to Europe. Looked at this way, there is no great mystery in the fact that the silliness of Lord Deepmeere and the fat Duchess, and even the crimes of the Bellegardes, are treated far less harshly in the novel than are the social ambitions of Noémie, Stanislas Kapp, and even the American hero himself.

Is *The American,* then, an American novel by virtue of its genre, as has sometimes been asserted? That, of course, depends first of all on the sort or novel one considers characteristically American and, second, on the sort of novel one takes *The American* to be. Have Americans typically written realistic novels, while their European colleagues wallowed in romanticism, as some theorists have maintained? Or is the realistic novel of manners, rather, an

English tradition and the American novel a romance, as we have so often been advised? Whichever line of argument we take, *The American* will both support and refute it. Newman is at once a more of less plausible type of the self-made American millionaire and a knight of chivalric romance in quest of his feminine ideal. The other characters are drawn both from James's own acquaintances in Paris and from books: legends, medieval romances, novels, and plays. The action in which these characters are engaged is both timelessly literary and historically topical. While almost everyone in the novel finds some occasion to remark upon the resemblance of the action to that of a play, a romance, or a poem, the story also reflects the rapidly changing conditions of political and social life in Europe: the deposing of the hereditary, landed nobility by the new aristocracy of industrial wealth; the increased social mobility of petits bourgeoises like Noémie and *commerçants* like Stanislas Kapp and Christopher Newman; the movement of Parisian life from the medieval *cité* on the Left Bank across the Seine to the new boulevards, the new commercial districts, and the *colonie Américaine* near the Arc de Triomphe; and, most important, the much larger shift, of which these others are only symptoms, of the center of Western civilization from the Old World to the New.

The setting of the novel is replete with verifiably accurate detail. Almost every building, street, and park that Newman visits can be found either in a copy of the guidebook that lies by his side on the divan of the Salon Carré or in the travel sketches James wrote for the *New York Tribune* during his stay in France. But in those moments when James manages to get inside the skin of his hero and see the world through his eyes, Paris becomes the landscape of Newman's evolving consciousness. These moments occur more and more frequently as the novel progresses and Newman begins to see in his surroundings not just an alien way of life but a projection of his own deepest desires and fears. And when the tone of the novel darkens with the frustration of his hopes, the open, luminous city of his original ambitions becomes a crepuscular gothic dungeon, the dark place in his own soul to which his attention is directed by the seemingly diabolical bafflement of his once boundless and unreflective self-confidence. In thus confounding the supposedly distinct realms of life and literature, the novel is neither simply realistic nor romantic but a "neutral territory," as Hawthorne said, "where the Actual and the Imaginary may meet and each imbue itself with the nature of the other."

Not even the theme of *The American*—the collision of disruptive American energy with repressive European tradition—can be called distinctively American. In the first place, the novel seems to be as interested in the differences between the Anglo-Saxon and Gallic "races" or between British moralism and French aestheticism as it is in the relative values of American and European culture and character. But even more important, the same thematic contest between energy and form that is enacted in *The American* can be found in nearly every literary work of consequence written in English in the nineteenth century. On this level of abstraction, the conflict between Newman's revolutionary ambitions and the Bellegardes' conservative formality is not fundamentally different from the contests between Blake's Orc and Urizen, Scott's Highlanders and Englishmen, Keats's Lamia and Apollonius, Hawthorne's Hester and Dimmesdale, Dickens's Dombey and Floy, Henry Adams's Dynamo and Virgin, and countless other literary versions of the great nineteenth-century debate concerning the relative value of permanence and change. Indeed, there are reasons to believe that James was more concerned with this fundamental conflict than he was with the particular metaphors in which it is expressed in *The American*. At the time that he wrote the novel, America stood in his mind not as realm of possibility but as the locus of his constrained and dependent youth. Europe was the open field, the land of opportunity, where he hoped to achieve his own personal and artistic identity. In *The Europeans,* written only a year after *The American,* it is the English visitors who are easygoing and morally elastic, while their American hosts are locked in the rigidities of New England tradition. Even in *The American* itself, the debate between energy and form has a way of detaching itself from its transatlantic geography and settling wherever James directs his attention. To Newman, Valentin's duel seems an image of European life in general: both barbarous and decadent, a blend of brutal, mindless passions and heartless social forms.

As an American novel that is not immediately distinguishable, on the basis of subject, style, argument, genre, or theme, from many of its European counterparts, *The American* calls into question the very idea of American literature. Although that idea has assumed various shapes over the years since Americans first decided that they should have their own literature as well as their own politics, it has always been an idea of *difference*. For all of the nineteenth-century journalists who, in calling upon their countrymen to create a truly American literature, tried to explain what it *should* be, and for all of the twentieth-century scholars and critics who have since tried to explain what it *is,* the aim has always been to establish between Europe and America a literary boundary as distinct as the Atlantic Ocean. This task has been both necessary and impossible for the same reason: what we call American literature simply does not have the sort of prima facie identity that the North American continent and the United States do. Even the most original and idiosyncratic works of American literature were written in a European language by persons steeped in transatlantic culture and whose idea of literature itself was based primarily upon European poetry, fiction, and drama. To be sure, the great American writers are unique. But great writing is unique by definition. Like writers everywhere, these Americans have cultivated uniqueness not so much to isolate themselves from the rest of the literary world, past and present, as to earn a place in that world by adding something new to it. Even Mark Twain and Whitman wanted seats in the literary pantheon, alongside Cervantes and Shakespeare, far more than they wanted a chapter in some future anthology of American literature. What is more, whenever some American has managed to do something unprecedented, something that might set American literature apart, his or her Euro-

pean colleagues have immediately incorporated this new development into their own work, thereby erasing the difference the
moment it appeared.

The more logical question to ask about American literature,
then, is not "What makes it *different*?" but "What *difference* has it
made?" How has it affected the course of modern literary history,
of which it has always been, willy-nilly, an inextricable part? To the
study of this question *The American* is especially well suited by
virtue of its peculiarly intimate connection with the personal life
and artistic development of the first American to be generally recognized as a major figure in a major international literary movement: the development of modern fiction. The idea for the novel
came to James (very much as the idea of quitting business and
going to Europe comes to Newman) while he was riding down
Broadway in a horsecar one day in the winter of 1874. James had
recently returned from one of the several extended tours that had
already occupied more than a quarter of his peripatetic youth. Not
long after he was born, in 1843, his father, the Swedenborgian
theologian for whom Henry was named, took him and his older
brother William, who was to become the great American prag-
matic philosopher, abroad to escape the limitations of provincial
culture and education. For the next thirty years, James divided his
time between Europe, where he traveled at first with his family
and then alone, and such American bastions of Old World culture
as Washington Place and Newport, where he changed schools and
tutors repeatedly, and Cambridge, where he studied the law and
began, in 1864, to publish reviews, stories, and critical essays in
the literary quarterlies.

Having just completed *Roderick Hudson,* his second novel and
the first to employ the international theme essayed in such earlier
tales as "A Passionate Pilgrim" and "An International Episode,"
James was determined to make his living as a writer. For the time
being, that meant hackwork for the journals and newspapers, but
he longed for the day when, like Newman, he could give up the
commercial life and seek a richer fortune in Europe. After many

delays, that day finally came in the fall of 1875, when James left New York for an indefinite stay in Paris. By the following April, he was at work on *The American,* the character of Christopher Newman having arisen in his mind, exactly as that personage does in the novel, "on a perfect day of the divine Paris spring, in the great gilded Salon Carré of the Louvre."

Although James later remembered writing the novel "off the top of his head," the period of composition appears to have been a particularly anxious time for him. To cover the expense of his European venture, the novel would have to be a popular success. To justify his contention that he could do better work by leaving America, it would have to be a critical success as well. The rightness of the most difficult and ultimately controversial decision he would ever make hung on the outcome of *The American.* Little wonder, then, that the novel reflects some of these anxieties. When the first installment appeared in the June 1876 issue of *The Atlantic Monthly,* the later chapters were not yet written, and James and his hero were both beginning to feel very much at home in Paris. But by the time the last installment came out, twelve months later, Newman had been rejected by the Bellegardes, and James had come to realize that he too would never be admitted into what he considered real Parisian society. The first American edition of the novel was hardly in the reviewers' hands when James abandoned the "detestable American Paris" to settle in London.

With *The American* and his Parisian difficulties behind him, James began the literary career that was to carry him initially into the popularity and critical esteem he longed for and then far beyond his readers and reviewers alike into an unmapped region of novelistic art that would remain largely unsettled well into the present century. In a very important sense, however, *The American* was not behind him at all, for at each major stage of that increasingly lonely career, Newman's story would reappear in a guise appropriate to the occasion. Just as the conception, composition, and serial publication of the novel had accompanied the anxious process of expatriation, the generally favorable reception of its first American edition started James on his brief rise to popularity. The first English edition appeared in 1879, alongside the hugely successful *Daisy Miller,* which made him famous by making his American heroine notorious, and his critical biography of Nathaniel Hawthorne, which announced James's literary farewell to America and his entry into London society. The inclusion of *The American* in the first uniform edition of his fiction, printed in London in 1883, marks his arrival at artistic and personal maturity following the completion of his first acknowledged masterpiece, *The Portrait of a Lady* (1881), and his long-postponed decision, upon the death of his parents in 1882, to reside permanently abroad.

A decade later, when James turned from fiction to the drama in hopes of securing both his reputation and his finances with a great theatric success, he began by turning *The American* into a play. And as the novel had heralded his rise to popularity and critical reputation, the play signaled a decline that would continue virtually unchecked until more than a decade after his death in 1916. The novels of the 1890s—*The Tragic Muse, The Spoils of Poynton, The Sacred Fount*—repelled readers by developing the forbidding "scenic" style that he had learned in the theater and would combine with the international theme of *The American* to produce the three great novels of his last, "major phase"—*The Wings of the Dove* (1902), *The Ambassadors* (1903), and *The Golden Bowl* (1904). In 1905, after revisiting America for the first time in more than twenty years, James rewrote *The American* one last time, revising it extensively in the style of these masterpieces for inclusion in the New York Edition of his works, his final attempt to regain the American reading public he had long since left behind.

At each of these crucial stages of his progress, James appears to have felt the need to rescue *The American* from the receding past by bringing it abreast of the latest development in his art and to renew his contacts with his American beginnings. It is as if each new departure revealed a new significance in this early novel, uncovering a new debt that increasing artistic mastery owed to an American apprenticeship. Although James paid the debt promptly each time it came due, the sense of continuing obligation clearly puzzled him, for to each reworking of the novel he attached a condescending, sometimes openly contemptuous, account of what seemed to him its artistic weaknesses. What could the infinitely delicate maneuverings of Lambert Strether's moral consciousness owe to the bold strokes of Newman's impulsive good nature, or the rich ambiguities of *The Golden Bowl* to the melodramatic simplicities of *The American*? How could this vindication of American generosity have set James on the path to Europe, and how could that path, from the New World to the Old, have led him to the future of the novel rather than back into its romantic past?

To retrace this journey is to negotiate the passage from the idea of America as something necessarily *different* from the rest of the world to that of its having made a *difference* in the whole world. Although the contest between Newman's modern energies and the Bellegardes' ancient formality does not distinguish James's novel from most of the important fiction and poetry written in England throughout the nineteenth century, the theme is nevertheless American in that the debate over the relative primacy and value of these two opposed ideas was precipitated by the discovery of America. It arose in the Renaissance as a quarrel between the "Ancients" and the "Moderns" concerning the ability of established forms of knowledge to accommodate this new and original discovery, and it grew increasingly urgent throughout seventeenth and eighteenth centuries as the tide of revolutionary energies loosed by the discovery gradually undermined the structures of knowledge and belief that had sustained Western civilization for nearly two thousand years. By the time James arrived on the scene in the 1870s the struggle had reached its crisis. In Europe and in America alike, the forces of reaction had retired behind the barricades of traditional belief, while the modern barbarians proceeded to sack the palaces of government, religion, and art.

Given the historical origins of James's theme, his dramatization
of it as the invasion of a feudal barony by a democratic American
adventurer seems wonderfully appropriate. What keeps it from
seeming peculiarly American is that the contest between Old
World forms and New World energies is resolved in the novel
entirely on Old World terms. If the Bellegardes wrong Newman
by reverting to their ancient principles, he triumphs over them by
refusing to pursue his ambition beyond the bounds of his conscience. American "good nature" manifests itself not in a decisive
action that creates its own moral value but in a refusal to act, and
it is no accident that Newman's decision is wholly agreeable to the
Bellegardes. The resolution is old-worldly in a structural sense as
well. In surrendering his power over the Bellegardes to the moral
form of his "good nature," Newman shapes his actions to the
moral form that James imposed upon the novel long before he
wrote it. Although Newman discovers the limits of his good nature in his desire for revenge, he cannot overstep those limits if
the novel is to arrive at its conclusion with its moral, the superiority of American conscience, still in hand.

That James should have conceived his American tale in this Old
World form is perfectly understandable. At that moment, he was
preparing to flee America for Europe, a place that held powerful
and complex associations for him. Like most of his American and
European contemporaries, James thought of the Old World and
the New as essentially different places: the Old World as the un-
altered past, the world as it was before the discovery of America,
and the New World as a radical departure from that past, with no
ties to it. According to this geography, Europe might provide
either a fixed point from which to measure modern progress or a
place to escape the drift of modern history. In either case, it constituted a timeless standard against which the history of the New
World could be judged. What is more, having been taught from
infancy to identify America with commerce and Europe with art,
James quite naturally associated art more closely with traditional
forms than with energetic actions. Ideally, he knew, art should

achieve a perfect fusion of form and action, a marriage of the Old and New worlds. But since the proof of Newman's character depends on his losing Claire, and since James knew from the beginning that they would make "an impossible couple," Newman must achieve that reconciliation on his own, by showing that his conscience restrains evil actions even more effectively than do the traditions of the Bellegardes.

At the same time, there runs throughout the controlling form of *The American* a powerfully subversive energy that continually threatens to do what James would one day insist a novel *should* do: burst the settled bounds of the author's prior intentions and propel the action beyond the well-kept paths of literary convention into the unpredictable, morally ambiguous world we actually inhabit. Although Newman manages to retain the good nature required by the foreordained outcome and moral of the story, James would never forget the effort this consistency had cost him. For Newman is by his very nature inconsistent. As Claire tells him, "You were born—you were trained to changes." Like Christopher Columbus, for whom he is named, and the Elizabethan merchant-adventurers, to whom he is often compared, Newman is one of those daring entrepreneurs whose ambition is to change the world and his own place in it. Like them, he does not conform to the world. He invents and perpetually reinvents it in the process of exploring it, inventing and reinventing himself with each new discovery until he comes at last to see that this unfolding world is both the cause and adequate symbol of his own evolving soul. As an agent of change, Newman is less a static type of American character than an enaction of the American consciousness, that curious, energetic, ambitious, and infinitely elastic spirit of moral originality that was loosed upon the Old World by the discovery of the New.

The result of this conflict between the static moral form of the novel and its energetic moral action is some confusion about Newman's true nature and what he is supposed to represent. On the one hand, we can only commend his refusal to blackmail the

Bellegardes. The national reputation for fair play is perfectly safe in his keeping. On the other hand, we may feel that his "good nature" is also his greatest weakness. Newman makes his final pilgrimage from the new, American Paris on the Right Bank, across the dark river, and into the underworld of the medieval *cité,* where his Ideal lies entombed because he desired her. But he returns empty-handed because he cannot violate his good nature to save her. The modern reader will not easily forgive Newman the precious "good nature" that is so necessary to his opinion of himself as a "good fellow wronged." Instead of insisting, against all evidence to the contrary, that he is "not wicked," he might better say, as does the American heroine of James's "Madame de Mauves": "I believe that if my conscience will prevent me from doing anything very base, it will effectually prevent me from doing anything very fine." The "fine" thing for Newman to do, surely, would be to acknowledge the baneful effect of his good nature on the lives of Noémie, Valentin, and Claire, and to sacrifice his good opinion of himself in order to repair some of the damage he has done. If he has used the letter, Mrs. Tristram assures him in the final scene, the Bellegardes would have capitulated and Claire might have been saved. That would not have been "good-natured," which is to say morally consistent, but it would have been "fine," which is to say morally beautiful. Above all, it would also be truer to Newman's actual "type," since no real American entrepreneur would hesitate for an instant to use his competitors' own weapons against them.

Looking back on *The American* from the end of his career, James that in making Newman consistent he had made the novel untrue and that in excluding all of those interesting complications upon which, he said, the art of the novel depends, he had made it inartistic. Far form reverting to their ancient principles, a real family of impoverished nineteenth-century aristocrats, he came to see, would have welcomed the rich American aboard with his gold. But that, James said, "wouldn't have been the theme of 'The American' . . . to which I was from so early pledged." If the

Bellegardes had given in, they would not be "Europeans," living embodiments of that Old World from which America had departed and to which both Newman and James sought to return. The old home, from which the Americans fell of their own accord (to paraphrase St. Augustine), would be seen to have fallen down while they were away from it. And if Newman blackmailed the Bellegardes, he would not be "good-natured." Instead of having produced a superior conscience, New World history would be seen to have departed from moral principle altogether. If the novel were true, in sum, there would be no moral forms at all, neither Old World traditions nor New World conscience, just selfish expediency on one side of the Atlantic and rapacious appetite on the other.

It is hardly surprising that *The American* cannot admit what it discovers, let alone explain it. James left America to escape the consequences of modern history, and the novel was written to justify his flight by demonstrating his American loyalty through European artistry. How could the novel tell this literally earth-shaking truth: that the Old World of timeless forms is gone, swept away by the tide of modern history? The Old World is unrecoverable because we have destroyed it and inescapable because we are forever to blame. The New Adam can neither redeem the past by harrowing hell, nor recover his original estate, nor escape the consequences of his willful fall, nor, by pursuing the course of his desires, arrive at that "New Heaven and New Earth" which is the old home in its final, perfect form. The Old World and the New are not different places—the one forever old and forever available, the other progressing toward moral perfection. There is only one world, forever new and forever old, a world of vagrant human energies without a source, a direction, or a destination to justify them.

The new world that *The American* helped James to discover would require a new conception of artistic form. Reflecting upon the novel when he turned it into a play, James said, "I will never again move in the strait-jacket of a novel conceived from a point wholly non-scenic . . . forcing one into a corner of forever keeping to it . . . and yet violating it at every step." Whereas Newman can "close the book" of his experience "and put it away," a fictive action that is true to life can never achieve its final form. "Really, universally," James came to see, "relations stop nowhere, and the exquisite problem of the artist is to draw, by a geometry of his own, the circle within which they shall happily appear to do so." This new form, in turn, would require a new conception of character—not an unchanging conscience opposed to action but an evolving consciousness inseparable from action. And the depiction of this consciousness would require a new kind of language, not a description of actions in moral terms but a morally symbolic action in its own right. *The American* had begun with a "non-scenic" moral plot that produced a necessarily consistent character. *The Portrait of a Lady* would begin with an unformed character whose life, unfolding out of her desires, would create the novel's plot. And *The Ambassadors* would begin with an imaginative consciousness, whose changes "from hour to hour" would constitute its action and its meaning, its energy and its form, at once. Although each of these developments would carry James further away from *The American,* he would describe the experience of writing these novels as the pursuit of "unforeseen developments" by a "rash adventurer" who has the necessary "courage" to face each "cruel crisis" in his story, "from the moment that he sees it grimly loom"—words that go a long way toward explaining his sense of continuing obligation to the problematic energies of Christopher Newman.

When James was virtually unknown, at work on his very first novel, he hoped it might become "the great American novel" that his countrymen were looking for. In the 1880s, at the peak of his popularity, he reaffirmed his ambition "to do something great," to "prove that I *can* write an American novel." And at the end of his life, with *The Ambassadors* behind him and his popularity beyond recall, he was still planning to write his "American novel." Since nothing he produced seems to have quite satisfied his idea of this national masterpiece, it is impossible to know exactly what he had in mind. We can be sure that he was not thinking of something like *Huckleberry Finn,* for he once stated his desire "to write in such a way that it would be impossible to say whether I am at any given moment an American writing about England or an Englishman writing about America." In James's view, a true American novelist would be one who could stand in "the company of Balzac or Thackeray"—although he did not mean, of course, that Americans should try to imitate those writers. He did not believe that this great American novel had ever been written. But when it did appear, he was sure, it would do more than satisfy America's craving for a national literature. It would contribute significantly to the art of the novel in general. "I think it not unlikely," he said at the very beginning of his career, "that American writers may yet indicate that a vast intellectual fusion and synthesis of the various National tendencies of the world is the condition of more important achievements than any we have seen. We must of course have something of our own—something distinctive and homogeneous—and I take it that we shall find it in our moral consciousness, our unprecedented spiritual lightness and vigour."

Measured against James's own standard, *The American* is less American than, say, Blake's *The Marriage of Heaven and Hell* or Carlyle's *Sartor Resartus,* both of which had caught the vigorous New World spirit of moral adventure and its powers of creative action. But if *The American* did not itself achieve that "vast intellectual fusion and synthesis" of Old World forms and New World energies, there is no doubt that the novel helped James to define the conditions of that achievement. The Henry James who wrote the novel was en route from the New World to the Old, but the novel he wrote was taking him from the Old World, in which legendary moral form and amoral human energy confronted each other across an estranging Atlantic, to the New World that was born with the discovery of America. Like the Newman who emerges from his Parisian adventure, the Henry James who emerges from the novel is neither an American nor a European in the old, differentiating sense. A sojourner in both places but at home in neither, he has risen above Old World geography into a lonely region where form and energy, detached from their native hemispheres, circle about each other endlessly in the powerfully energetic and highly formal dance of modern art.

American Writers and
English Literature

The idea of an American literature was conceived, late in the eighteenth century, to deal with a single, inescapable problem: the literature in question, when it finally appeared, would be written in English. If, as Walter Channing wished several decades later, the Revolution had only driven the English language out of America along with the British troops and erected in its place a linguistic counterpart to the new government,[1] our literary patriots would not have had to call for an American literature, argue about what form it should take, and then sit around wondering when it was going to appear. It would have come into being the minute someone wrote a literary work in the new language. With each subsequent production, it would have grown larger, and we would now have an American literature—whether good, bad, or indifferent—whose existence need never have been proclaimed, its proper contents debated, its differences from other literatures insisted upon, its rights to membership in the Modern Language Association disputed. Like French literature or Russian literature, it would exist independent of our statements on its behalf, simply by virtue of its language.

The mother tongue that necessitated the invention of American literature has been a constant embarrassment to her ungrateful offspring, which came into the world claiming political origins and have subsequently traced its bloodlines to institutions, climate, morals, ideals, culture, geography, psychology, and myth in an effort to deny its smothering linguistic parent. She has, however, proved immune to every spurning, largely because, for all of its protestations of independence, American literature has never really wanted to leave her. In the course of an argument against the nationalistic idea that American literature begins in 1776,

Howard Mumford Jones made a statement that few Americanists would now dispute. "American Literature," Jones said, "is as old as Jamestown."[2] But if geographical America, not the political United States, begat American literature, we may ask, why isn't it as old as San Salvador? The answer, of course, is that Columbus did not write in English. If we then ask why, since English seems to be a criterion after all, American literature should not be considered part of English literature, or why it should not at least include writings in English from Canada, the Caribbean, and elsewhere in the Americas, our attention is immediately directed away from the language, back to politics, where we began. English literature is written in England; American literature is "written in the United States," or, in the case of pre-Revolutionary American writings, "in the future United States."[3]

English, it seems, is something the idea of American literature can neither do with nor do without. If the language is explicitly acknowledged to be an essential element of that idea, it threatens to undercut all of those claims for autonomy and uniqueness upon which the idea rests. When, on the other hand, the linguistic element is ignored, criticism is deprived of its primary object, and the study of American literature becomes historical rather than literary. And if the linguistic criterion were to be removed altogether, American literature would immediately include works in all of the languages that American writers have ever employed—Asian, African, and aboriginal American, as well as European—and most Americanists would suddenly find themselves unqualified to study and teach the subject.

These questions about the relation of the English language to American literature are by no means new. They have simply not been raised in public since World War I, when American literature, having "come of age" and entered college, ceased to be a matter for debate and began to be taken for granted. From the time of the Revolution until the early decades of the twentieth century, however, American literature was a journalistic rather than an academic subject, and the journalists, having no professional stake in the subject, wondered repeatedly whether an American literature was possible without an American language. Noah Webster's belief, expressed in the 1780s, that "America must be as independent in *literature* as she is in *politics*" was closely tied to his conviction that "as an independent nation, our honor requires us to have a system of our own in language as well as in government." A quarter century later, John Pickering thought he could discern enough progress toward the development of an American language to presage a day when American writers would find themselves unable to read Milton, and their works would be unintelligible to English audiences. For Pickering's less conservative contemporaries, however, the progress was altogether too slow. America's intellectual dependence, Hugh Legaré and J. W. Simmons wrote in 1829, still awaited the formation of *"a dialect of our own"*; while Henry Wheaton, writing in 1824, concurred in the earlier judgment of Walter Channing that the tardy emergence of an American literature was entirely owing to the want of an American language.[4]

By midcentury, feelings of disappointment like Wheaton's and of trepidation like Pickering's conspired to diminish the expectation that American writing would ever cease to be English. To John Neal, American literature was "a phase of English literature—that literature which is put forth in the English language on both sides of the water." England and America, Alexander Everett maintained, "must always, in a literary view, be regarded as one great community," and W. H. Prescott felt that, owing to the common language of the two countries, "our literature can only be a variety of theirs." Fitz-Greene Halleck refused to call American literature anything but "American specimens of English literature" because, he said, "I have never been able to find out what *American literature* means." In Howells's view, it could only mean "a condition of English literature," although this fact was not necessarily a cause for regret. As T. Watts put the case in 1891, "The fine work of the poets of America shows, not that there is any probability that a national poetry will ever be developed, but that

English poetry will be enriched by English writers born on American soil." And in 1910, Brander Matthews concluded that "the relation between the British branch of English literature and the American branch must ever be intimate; and there is disadvantage in considering the one without keeping the other in mind always."[5]

Although such doubts concerning the possibility of America's literary independence from the rest of the English-speaking world could still be heard as late as 1915,[6] they were soon drowned out in the roar of national pride that greeted the American military triumph in Europe. Alongside America's new image of itself as an independent world power, there emerged a critical consensus that, over the years since the Revolution, Americans had in fact managed to produce a number of world-class writings and that together these constituted an autonomous American literature, their language notwithstanding.[7] The war with English, however, was not yet won. When, emboldened by this idea of America's literary autonomy, a group of progressive academics sought to introduce American literature into the university curriculum, they quite naturally applied first to the departments of English, which had themselves, along with the other modern languages, only recently gained a measure of scholarly recognition after an extended struggle against the Classicists. At the time, however, the study of English was almost entirely philological—which is to say, linguistic—and just as American writings had been kept out of the colleges a century before because they were written in English rather than in Latin or Greek, they were excluded now because, being written in English, and modern English at that, they added nothing to the list of exemplary texts through which the rise of modern English was normally traced. Only on some ground other than language could American literature base its claims of autonomy, and neither the typical English department nor the Modern Language Association was yet prepared to accept such extralinguistic claims.[8]

Denied recognition by departments of English, American writings found their first academic home in departments of history, where the word "American" designated a recognized political entity—the United States of America—and a book written in English could be considered American as long as its author was a citizen and its subject had some apparent relation to life in America. The study of American literature prospered in this congenial setting, establishing the canon of truly "American" books, refining the definitions of their Americanness, tracing the historical lines that connected them, and eventually producing, under the ambiguous rubric of "American Civilization," a number of doctoral theses and monographs of a decidedly literary stripe.[9] During this same period, the old philological structure of English studies was gradually being replaced by courses in literature, including, in certain rare instances, a course or two on the "Chief American Writers."[10] And with the opening of this bridge between the more humanistic wings of American Studies and the English departments, the Americanists crossed over and set up camp among the professors of English—only to discover that they had pitched their tent in a nest of Anglophiles, for whom "English" had come to mean "British," and "American" to mean "literarily second rate."[11]

This hostile climate was to prove unexpectedly salubrious, for the newly assumed equation of "English" and "British" enabled American literature to preserve the national identity it had acquired from its association with American history. Had "English" continued to denote a language, as it did when the English departments were founded, that identity would have instantly evaporated, and there would now be no departments of "English and American Literature" offering degrees in this politically divided subject, let alone in one or the other of its national compartments. But as the English curriculum shifted its emphasis from racial philology to national literary history and then to stateless literary criticism, the old linguistic problem of American literature vanished from sight. As far as the historians of British literature were concerned, American literature was American all right but not very literary. In the view of the cosmopolitan critics, American literature might include a handful of literary works, but these belonged to world literature, not to America. Suspended between these two warring factions of the modern English department, American literature could at last fulfill the dream of its earliest framers and be both American and literary without having either to abandon or apologize for its language.

And yet this conspiracy of silence could not make the problem go away. As long as American literature was written in a language not its own, it would have to go on searching for some other way to distinguish itself from the rest of the English-speaking literary world or else give up its claims to autonomy altogether. Viewed in this light, the theories of American literature that have issued from the university presses over the last half-century or more seem merely to restate in academic terms the journalistic debate of the previous century. Like their journalistic forebears, the professors of American literature have sought its uniqueness in its subjects (social manners, frontier individualism), its forms (the romance, the free-verse poem), its themes (the fall from innocence, the recovery of paradise), and its modes of representation (realism, symbolism). Venturing dangerously close to the precincts of language itself, they have even tried to locate the uniqueness of American literature in its "style." But none of these literary substitutes for an American language has ever managed to win unanimous acceptance. For not only are they often mutually contradictory, but some troublemaker has always been able to find, in each case, at least one major American work that does not display the supposedly definitive literary feature and any number of non-American works that do.[12]

Not surprisingly, many theorists have preferred to seek this substitute for American language in American history rather than in American literary traits. It was in departments of history, we recall, that the earliest academic theories of American literature were framed. What is more, when books are thought of as literary objects, they tend to flee their places of origin and associate themselves with their generic, thematic, structural, and stylistic counterparts from other countries. When they are regarded as historical events, on the other hand, they tend to remain rooted in the geographic, political, or cultural soil that gave them birth. Once *The Scarlet Letter* has been described as a book about New England, written in New England by a native New Englander, it needs no dubious demonstration of literary uniqueness to seem American. The difficulty here is that if the literary substitutes for language have failed to establish the Americanness of American literature, the historical alternative has tended to leave its literariness almost entirely out of account. The American works that most clearly reflect their cultural and political circumstances—"The Song of Hiawatha," say, or *The Man Without a Country*—often turn out to be the least noteworthy in any literary respect, while such literarily important works as Emily Dickinson's poetry or *The Confidence-Man* may be perfectly unrepresentative of their place and time. To be sure, certain theorists have cut this knot by simply equating literary and historical importance—either letting historical considerations identify the classics, as V. L. Parrington did, or taking Lionel Trilling's advice and allowing critical standards to decide which works the cultural historian should read.[13] But these solutions have only obscured the problems that necessarily beset every attempt to create an American literature in the absence of an American language.

The tacit agreement among scholars of American literature to study only works written in English and, at the same time, to forget that they are written in English has led to a great deal of nonsense. It is often supposed that by crossing the Atlantic and then rebelling against the Crown the British colonists cut themselves off from English literary culture and had to begin the work of constructing ex nihilo an America tradition to take its place.[14] According to this cataclysmic theory, someone like Charles Brockden Brown, having no American predecessors, is necessarily an original. Anything he did may be considered American since an American did it, and any subsequent American novelist who did something similar becomes Brown's direct descendant. Distinguished by their common nationality and bound together by certain literary resemblances among their works, these writers are said to constitute a tradition, which can only be attributed to American culture and must therefore be characteristically, representatively, and uniquely American.

This rickety edifice might lead one to infer that its architects were simply ignorant, unacquainted with both the literary and the historical worlds in which the major American writers actually lived. The case is, rather, that while scholars of American literature possess this knowledge in abundance, they cannot use it without seriously weakening the foundation on which their subject rests: the idea that American literature is written in English but is not English literature.[15] Although the substitution of "American" for "English" automatically makes American literature a historical subject, scholars of American literature cannot really be historians, for they cannot acknowledge a number of well-known historical facts related to language: that Anglo-America and England have always constituted a single, complex, English-speaking culture; that Americans have written in many languages other than English; and that, both historically and geographically, the boundaries of the United States embrace only part of Anglo-American culture.[16] By the same token, although scholars of American literature aspire to be literary critics, they cannot freely employ two of the principal contexts in which any literary work is normally described and explained: the language in which the work is written and other works written in the same language. Little wonder that the study of American literature has a reputation, among historians and critics alike, for theoretical incoherence, methodological laxity, unrestrained generalization, and provincialism.

The effects of this political subdivision of English literature upon the study of British writing, although perhaps less obvious, have been no less baneful. While scholarship in British literature of the sixteenth and seventeenth centuries has begun to pay closer attention to English writings from the New World (even as a new generation of specialists in "Early American Literature" has begun to claim more and more of these materials for "the future United States"), Anglo-American writings seldom figure in studies of the British eighteenth century, and from the time of the American Revolution to the rise of international modernism after World War I, American and British literature are customarily viewed as inhabiting two almost totally unrelated realms.[17] Taking exceptionalist theories of American literature at face value and equating a scorn for American things with the acquisition of elegant culture, critics of British literature—even those who are Americans themselves—have managed to dismiss from consideration a collection of works whose influence on individual British writers and on the overall development of British writing was demonstrably profound. Like their Americanist counterparts, the critics of British literature may know the facts—what George Eliot, Clough, Froude, Arnold, John Sterling, Herbert Spencer, John Tyndall, and Thomas Huxley thought of Emerson, for example, or what Tennyson, Swinburne, D. G. Rossetti, Yeats, and Gosse thought of Poe—but they cannot use this information without inconveniently blurring the political boundaries they have drawn around their literary subject. As a result, they cannot adequately account for such significant events in British literary history as the recrudescence of "romanticism" among the Modernists after its long "Victorian" sleep.[18]

These limitations on historical scholarship and literary criticism suggest that the profession of English is paying too high a price for the quaint pleasures of self-regarding anglophilia and misplaced American patriotism. There is no reason to forget that Cooper was an American, that Scott was a Briton, and that their respective political, geographical, and social situations helped to condition what they wrote. But neither is there any reason to forget that they both wrote novels in English for an international audience and that these literary circumstances conditioned their writings no less. Indeed, because we are literary scholars first and historians of culture, or society, or ideas only in the service of literary knowledge, we should define our subject in literary terms—language, genre, theme, structure, and style—before we begin to subdivide it along political or geographical lines. Once we have decided to study literature in English, whether our favorite writers happen to be Britons or Americans, our subject has already been defined for us, as literature first of all, then as literature in English; and no further specification of these categories by place or period will remove us from them. For the historian, *Leaves of Grass* may be an important moment in American culture; for the literary scholar, it is a significant event in the development of English literature, and neither that work nor that development can be literarily understood apart from each other.

To put the case in the words of George Routledge's announcement for his *Broadway* magazine in 1868: "We are convinced that there is a still Broader way for Literature and Art than that which spreads itself under the shadow of St. Paul's in London, or stretches from the Battery to Harlem Bridge in New York."[19] Admittedly, the proposition that all literature in English, including that written by Americans, is English literature has never been very well received, especially in America, where it has often been associated either with anglophilia or racism. But insofar as "English" is taken literally, to denote a language, rather than historically, to denote a nationality, American writings lose nothing by their inclusion in this literary subject. On the contrary, it is only within this context that their true literary importance can be determined. Nor does the proposition necessarily imply that American culture is essentially Anglo-Saxon, as the English philologists were inclined to believe. For it is only when we stop identifying American literature and American writings in English that American writings in other languages will take their rightful place in American studies. Indeed, if anglophilia and racism are truly our concerns, we would do well to scrap our present system, with its assumed equations of English literature with British writings and of American literature with writings in English. But whatever costs to British and American national pride may follow from our decision to take up the study of English literature, they will be more than repaid by our newly won freedom to face a large number of well-known but heretofore unmentionable facts.

The first of these facts is that the British have been intensely interested in America ever since its discovery, and this interest has grown steadily over the centuries with the magnitude of America itself, the volume of printed materials concerning it, and the number of Britons capable of reading these materials. In the sixteenth century, the reports of the New World voyagers were not only widely read in themselves, they exerted a powerful influence on Tudor poetry, drama, and fiction.[20] Following the planting of the British colonies in the seventeenth century and the large-scale migration of Britons to the New World, increasing numbers of books written by American colonists began to appear in England. Many of these were written expressly for British audiences and originally published there, while those that were published first in the colonies were often either reprinted in England or imported by London booksellers.[21] With the increasing flow of written words from west to east in the eighteenth century, "America" became a common metaphor of social, material, and intellectual aspiration that fed itself on news from the New World in the popular press. Regular reports on colonial affairs began to appear in British periodicals, including enthusiastic reviews of such American works as Jefferson's *Notes on the State of Virginia*, Imlay's *Topographical Description* . . . , Bartram's *Travels* . . . , Trumbull's "M'Fingal," and the poems of Richard Lewis, David Humphreys, and Joel Barlow. Franklin's works were more widely read in England than in America. The novels of Royall Tyler and Charles Brockden Brown were better received there than they were at home. By the end of the century, in fact, the British interest in American writings had become sufficiently widespread to occasion two bibliographies of Americana for English readers, as well as a rising chorus of calls upon the new nation to produce an indigenous literature of its own.[22]

In the nineteenth century, the British appetite for American writings became simply voracious.[23] During this period, Britons read more books by Americans than by the authors of all other foreign nations combined and knew more about America than they did about any other country. Cooper and W. E. Channing were as well known in England as any of their British contemporaries. Irving was more popular there than Lamb, and John Murray paid more for *The Conquest of Granada* than for the first installment of *Don Juan*. Longfellow's books sold more copies than Tennyson's, and *Uncle Tom's Cabin* alone outsold anything by Scott, Dickens, or Bulwer. The bulk of the market for cheap books and for juvenile literature was supplied by American writers, and of the four works most often found in the homes of working-class readers late in the century, two—Stowe's *Uncle Tom's Cabin* and Susan Warner's *Wide, Wide World*—were by Americans.

In their eagerness to see America develop its own literature, British reviewers scolded Americans for failing to appreciate the work of their countrymen. The charge was quite just in that Hawthorne, Longfellow, Poe, Melville, and Brown were all better received in England than in their own country. *Representative Men, Moby-Dick, The Marble Faun, Huckleberry Finn,* some thirty titles by Cooper, six by Irving, and a dozen or more by Longfellow were all published first in England. Irving and Melville were taken seriously first by British critics. Brown was receiving favorable attention from Godwin, Scott, Shelley, and Keats while he was being largely ignored in America. And his novels, like Melville's, remained in print in England long after they had been forgotten in the United States. Hardy and William Archer were the first readers to say that *Huckleberry Finn* was something more than a piece of literary clowning. Hawthorne was praised extravagantly by Fitzgerald, George Eliot, and Meredith, recommended by Jowett, and considered by Arnold an even better writer than Emerson, whose *Essays* he nevertheless adjudged the most important English prose of the age.

The fact is, quite simply, that throughout the nineteenth century American writing constituted a central element of British literary life. Coleridge, as we know, made significant use of Imlay, Bartram, and the early voyage narratives; and Wordsworth was said to have known Bartram by heart. Between 1880 and 1900 alone British publishers brought out nine editions of works of Melville, twenty by Whitman and Thoreau, twenty-five by Emerson and Whittier, thirty-five by Lowell and Cooper, sixty by Irving and Mark Twain, seventy by Holmes, and ninety by Hawthorne. Among the many British writers who acknowledged the direct influence of some American were Kingsley, Arnold, George Eliot, D. G. Rossetti, Robert Louis Stevenson, Conan Doyle, Conrad, Symonds, Kipling, Clough, and Froude. And the first book-length studies of Whitman, Emerson, Holmes, Thoreau, Poe, and Longfellow were all written by British critics for British readers, who considered these American authors, quite rightly, part of their own literary culture.

The second fact to be faced by the student of English literature is that until well along in the nineteenth century Americans in general read more books written by Britons than by their fellow Americans and, even more important, that American writers continued to do so until after World War I. In the seventeenth century, when most of the American colonists considered England their home and the colonies individually were apt to be in closer contact with England than with each other, British books made up the bulk of every colonial library. Throughout the colonial period, the great majority of books offered for sale in American cities were written by Englishmen, and Americans constituted a large part of the readership for the periodical literature that has been called "the most important missionary of British culture" abroad. Far from desiring to throw off the chains of British influence, the colonial writer was often at pains to keep the channels of transatlantic communication open. Those, like William Byrd, who were fortunate enough to visit England made a special effort to meet their British colleagues, and Franklin took it upon himself to promote the sale of British books in the colonies.[24]

If these facts tend to confirm the traditional image of a colonial culture tied to its maternal apron strings, corresponding data from the nineteenth century seriously discredit the notion that American writers threw off these ties after the Revolution. To be sure, the corridors of journalism rang with cries for an American literature free from the pernicious influences of Addison, Pope, Byron, and Scott. But these lamentations attest as much to the popularity and continuing influence of these writers as to any desire on the part of American readers or authors to escape that influence. Had Americans not found Byron linguistically accessible and culturally congenial, no nationalist critic would have needed to condemn this unpatriotic taste. The fact is, however, that a poll taken to discover the favorite authors of nineteenth-century American writers would turn up very few American names. Brown placed Shakespeare, Godwin, and Mary Wollstonecraft above any American writer. Irving's initial devotion to Addison and Goldsmith shifted in time to Scott, Byron, and Campbell. John Quincy Adams thought Nahum Tate the equal of nine Bryants. Emerson called Coleridge and Carlyle his teachers. Poe called Tennyson "the poet of poets." Hawthorne wished he could write like Trollope. Whitman confessed that Scott permeated him and his poetry "through and through." When Emily Dickinson listed "her books" for Thomas Higginson, she named Keats, the Brownings, Ruskin, Thomas Browne, and Revelations (King James Version), pointedly excluding Whitman. And Melville produced his American classic immediately upon reading Shakespeare, Burton, Browne, Carlyle, and De Quincey.

If it is true that American writers were neglected in their own country, the reason appears to be not that Americans were too busy to read, as it is often said, but that they were too busy reading British authors. Americans bought more copies of works by Dickens and Tennyson than Britons did. Charles Reade estimated that his American following exceeded his British public threefold. Carlyle and Tennyson found more favor, early in their careers, among American critics than in the British reviews. George Eliot, Meredith, Hardy, Shaw, Galsworthy, and Wells were all better received in America than at home. And the first collected editions of Cud-worth, Bolingbroke, Paley, Burke, Dugald Stewart, and Macaulay were all prepared by American scholars. So pronounced, in fact, was the American interest in British literary culture that Americans often wrote with the British reader in mind. Irving, Cooper, Hawthorne, Bret Harte, Crane, James, and Henry Adams all spent a part of their productive lives in England; and knowing that the British reviews of their work often determined its American reception, Mark Twain, Bret Harte, Howells, and James quite consciously tailored their writings for the British reader. In the words of Richard Rush, England formed an unavoidable part of the American writer's mental landscape: "In the nursery he learns her ballads. Her poets train his imagination. Her language is his with its whole intellectual riches, past and forever newly flowing; a tie, to use Burke's figure, light as air, and unseen; but stronger than links of iron."

The conclusion to be drawn from these facts of mutual literary interest is that, whatever their nationalities may have been, as writers these Britons and Americans lived in the same literary country.[26] Like their intellectual colleagues in philosophy and the sciences, they read each other's work and wrote with each other in mind. Many of them knew each other personally or carried on extended friendly correspondences—Wordsworth and Ticknor, Carlyle and Emerson, George Eliot and Stowe, Fitzgerald and Lowell, Tennyson and Tuckerman, Rossetti and Whitman, Mark Twain and Browning, Barrie and Cable. In many respects, they shared more in common with each other than with their local readers, literarily unsophisticated as these tended to be in both countries, or with those cultural watchdogs among their own countrymen who habitually ascribed every unfamiliar, and therefore unwelcome, literary development to pernicious influences from across the Atlantic. For these writers, as for their political compatriots, the words "British" and "American" often designated not two separate places but rather two opposed temperaments that were manifest in both places. To conservatives like Ar-

nold and Pickering, "British" meant "traditionally ordered,"
"American" meant "anarchic"; while to radicals like Blake and Jefferson the words meant "moribund" on the one hand and "ener-
getically progressive" on the other. Regarded in this context, not
even the idea of American literature is strictly American, since it
was compounded largely from reactions against "foreign" neoclassicism (which the American nativists called "British" and the British called "French"), Edward Young's thoughts on originality, and
Hugh Blair's individualist aesthetics and was a matter of considerable interest to progressive Britons as well as to American literary nationalists.[27]

The common world that unites the British and the American
writer, transcending all geographical and political divisions, is the
world of written English. This language is dialectally and stylisti-
cally diverse, to be sure. Diversity, however, is one of its essential
characteristics, and the differences between British and American
writings are no more pronounced than those among the writers
of either country.[28] No one would ever suppose that a Briton
wrote "Song of Myself" or *Huckleberry Finn*. But neither would
anyone suppose that the same person wrote those two works and
Moby-Dick as well. Mark Twain's language is closer to Dickens's
than to Melville's, whose own literary style is closer to De Quincey's than to either Whitman's or Twain's. Equally important, the
language that binds together the works of Chaucer and Pope, of
Burns and Artemus Ward, of Dickinson and Cooper, making
them all equally intelligible to any literate English-speaker, also
divides them from writings in other languages across a gulf that
only translation can bridge. The differences between the languages or Poe and Thackeray are very great, but they are nothing
compared to the differences between their language and Flaubert's
or Goethe's. We cannot imagine Chekhov using Johnson's dictionary, but Charles Brockden Brown did; while for most
nineteenth-century Britons the common term for dictionary was
"Webster's." Collections of English verse complied in Britain
commonly included American poems at the time when Rufus

Griswold proclaimed John Milton a more essentially American writer than any who had yet appeared in the United States. And Lowell was nominated for the first professorship of English literature at Oxford not very many years before D. H. Lawrence proved himself the most able interpreter of American literature.

No less striking than the structural uniformity that makes English, amid all its diversity, a single language is its flexibility, its capacity for assimilating new elements and for adapting to new circumstances. And of all of the situations that have altered the language over the past four centuries, surely the most significant is the extension of English-speaking culture across the Atlantic to the New World. Historians of the language commonly date the beginning of modern English at 1500, alongside the discovery of America and the appearance of those printed books through which the discovery was realized and fostered.[29] With the planting of the first British colonies in North America, a century later, unprecedented demands were placed on the language as writers like John Smith struggled to formulate an idiom that would both accurately represent conditions in the New World and meet the linguistic standards of authority in force at home. From that time on, English has evolved principally by way of a dialogue between the Old World and the New. Just as the American colonies transformed England by financing her industrial revolution, which in turn transformed America, the colonial experience transformed her language by introducing new words, new verb forms, new syntactical standards, which in turn made possible those new social identities, political institutions, and conceptions of reality that transformed the colonies into an independent nation. And just as the demographic, economic, and political center of the English-speaking world shifted gradually from east to west during the nineteenth century, the linguistic forces of change associated with America—plainness, stylistic leveling, neologisms, the enfranchisement of the vernacular—gradually overcame the linguistic principles of ordered stability associated with Britain—eloquence, stylistic hierarchy, correctness—eventually producing that twentieth-century phenomenon called "the Americanization of English."

It must be emphasized that while much of the impetus for this development came from America, the development itself has been uniform throughout the English-speaking world. At the same time that Webster was contemplating the effects of spreading the English language over the entire North American continent, the Englishman Thomas Pownall was writing: "North America is become *a new primary planet* in the system of the world, which, whilst it takes its own course in its own orbit, must have effect on the orbit of every other planet and SHIFT the common centre of gravity of the whole system of the European world."[30] Fifty years later, while Emerson was predicting the literary consequences of this gravitational shift, *Blackwood's Magazine* was observing that "the current sets in strong and fast from the Transatlantic shores, and the old Bulwarks of England are fast giving way before its fury." Lowell considered the American vernacular a force that would keep the English language alive and growing, and Henry James foresaw the day when every European writer would have to take America into account. But such views were by no means peculiar to Americans. William Archer maintained that "America has greatly enriched the language," and Virginia Woolf fulfilled James's prediction in saying that, to describe the modern English-speaking world, "a new tradition is needed and the control of a new tradition. That both are in process of birth the language itself gives proof. For the Americans are doing what the Elizabethans did—they are coining new words. They are instinctively making the language adapt itself to their needs."[31]

Although the reigning theory of American literature as an independent, autochthonous, unique collection of writings with a history of its own appears to be little more than a political fiction, concocted in defiance of the literary facts, that theory can also be regarded, more charitably, as a crude way of expressing the perception that American writers have contributed significantly to the development of English literature. There is, at any rate, no other way to explain the present canon of major American writings. Emerson's essays, *The Scarlet Letter, Moby-Dick, Huckleberry Finn*, the poems of Whitman and Dickinson have not been singled out for our attention because they are more uniquely or characteristically or representatively American than, say, *Gates Ajar* and *The Biglow Papers*. They were cut from the common herd because they are literarily more important—which is to say, important to literature, rather than to America. Once selected for their literary value, of course, these masterworks have been arranged into any number of purportedly unique "American traditions." But these retroactively imposed schemes are merely expressions of American cultural insecurity—the feeling that to be world champions we must play the national game—and they might simply be ignored if they did not tend to frustrate the very purposes they were designed, in part, to serve. The fact is, however, that the isolation of American classics from the rest of English literature actively prevents us from understanding, let alone explaining, their literary importance, which lies not in some supposed difference between them and their British counterparts, as theories of America literature would have it, but in the difference they have made in English literature as a whole.

Among the most significant developments in English literature over the last four hundred years, there are few, if any, that can be fully understood or explained without reference to writings from America. The emergence of the first-person voice, in both prose narrative and poetry, with its implications of individual worth, the authority of personal experience, the subjective dimension of reality, and the value of curiosity and ambition, is owing in large measure to the reports of the early voyagers, whose own words were the only evidence of the unprecedented wonders they had discovered. The development of a "scientific" prose style, rhetorically uncluttered, syntactically disciplined, and lexically precise, stems from the same source: the voyagers' need to describe things so that they could be found again, controlled, and turned to use.[32] The novel was invented to arbitrate the dispute between the

New World idea of reality as the product of human action and the Old World conception of the truth as an unalterable system of divinely instituted forms. The voyagers' exposure to exotic pagan cultures and beliefs led on the one hand to a revaluation of the primitive that lent poetic dignity to the language of rustics, commoners, and savages, and on the other hand to the view that all beliefs, including one's own, are fictions imposed upon the credulous by the powerful and hence to a modern rhetoric of relativism, intransigence, and irony.[33] The modern view of the artist as one obliged to choose between fame and excellence and the emergence of this choice as a dominant literary theme are directly attributable to social, political, and economic changes that were fostered throughout the Western world in the eighteenth and nineteenth centuries by the spread of ideas from and about America.[34] Indeed, the very idea of modernity, of the present and future as utterly divorced from the past, was born with the discovery that the shape and meaning of the world are radically unlike those envisioned by the ancient authorities.

So important is American writing in the history of English literature that the principal phases of this evolution may be said, not altogether fancifully, to coincide with major turning points in the course of England's relations with America. The medieval period extends to approximately 1500, when England learned of the discovery and began the long process of revising those antique conceptions of the world and of human destiny that the discovery had called into question. This period of ideological upheaval, known as the English Renaissance, covers the hundred years or so between the discovery and planting of the first British colonies in America, around 1600, not long after the composition of the first known document by an Englishman who had actually been to the New World. The period of the English Enlightenment, then, covers most of the seventeenth and eighteenth centuries, from the early settlement to the American Revolution, which was the culmination of Enlightenment thought and which set in motion those forces of intellectual, social, and political change that were to preoccupy the century to come. Lacking a catchword for this next period, we may call it simply the nineteenth century, the era in which the gravitational center of the English-speaking world shifted from the Old World to the New and which closed with the decisive American victory in World War I. This cataclysmic event, finally, announces the somewhat belated entry of English literature into the international Modern movement, which can be said really to have begun with the discovery of America and has at any rate not yet ended.

When the history of English literature is described in terms of Anglo-American rather than British events, not only its overall shape and direction but those of its component periods take on an unwonted coherence and clarity. Nineteenth-century English literature, for example, is customarily divided into three compartments—Romantic, Victorian, and American—which cannot possibly be reassembled to provide a clear picture of the whole period because they are formed on different logical principles. Romantic literature is writing of a certain *kind*. Victorian literature was written in a certain *time*. And American literature comes from a certain *place*. Worse yet, while these subcategories are not logically compatible, neither are they mutually exclusive, precluding the existence, say, of a Romantic poem written in America during the Victorian period. If, on the other hand, nineteenth-century English literature is regarded as all literature written in English between the American Revolution and World War I—whatever its kind, date, or place of origin—the period begins to display both a character that distinguishes it from its flanking periods and a tendency that proceeds from the Enlightenment to the Modern era and so connects them.

If our comprehension of English literary history depends upon our recognizing that American writings are an important part of it, our understanding of those American writings, depends, conversely, on our seeing them in this larger literary context. The ambiguous literary status of writings from British America before the Revolution is owing primarily to our thinking of them as

American rather than as English, as a primitive phase in the evolution of a truly "American" literature that was not complete until
the mid-nineteenth century. By viewing them in this political context, we simultaneously subject them to nineteenth-century criteria of literariness, which are quite inappropriate, and detach them
from the dynamic literary situation of the seventeenth century—
that is, from the very situation for which they were in large measure responsible and that was in turn ultimately responsible for
the character of nineteenth-century writing, British and American
alike. True enough, British America produced no poems, plays, or
novels that can compete for belletristic honors against the work of
Milton, Dryden, and Fielding. But it is also true that literary English changed more significantly between 1600 and 1775 than in
the previous seven centuries, and there is little reason to doubt
that the transportation of the English language to the New World
was one of the major causes of that change. The question is, which
procedure is more apt to reveal the true literary value of British-
American writing: isolating it from the rest of English literature
so that Wigglesworth must compete with Herbert on the one
hand and Whitman on the other, or including it in English literature so that William Strachey and John Josselyn can help to explain the literary changes that take us from Mallory and Thomas
Wyatt to Defoe and Thomas Gray?

Among the critical benefits that arise from our erasure of the
political divisions within English literature, the ability to trace literary developments of this sort is especially important. It is simply
impossible to explain the most significant literary features of
Moby-Dick without going outside the boundaries of the United
States, to the work of Shakespeare, Browne, Milton, Coleridge,
Carlyle, and De Quincey. As Cooper put it, "The authors, previously [*sic*] to the revolution are common property, and it is quite
idle to say that the American has not just as good a right to claim
Milton, and Shakespeare, and all the old masters of the language,
for his countrymen, as an Englishman."[35] By the same token, it is
impossible to explain the development of the novel from Scott

and Jane Austen to Conrad and Joyce without considering *Moby-Dick*, which exploded the novel form Melville had inherited. More than any other single writer, Melville epitomizes the course of English literature in the nineteenth century, from the Blakean celebrations of creative energy in *Mardi* to the Frostian accommodations to "a diminished thing" in the late poems. Irving supplies the missing link between the poetry of Byron and the prose of De Quincey; Emerson clarifies the kinship between Wordsworth and Arnold; Hawthorne marks the path that leads from Jane Austen to George Eliot; and Whitman smooths the way from Scott to Swinburne. But Melville alone bestrides the entire nineteenth century—from the unabashed "romanticism" of *Mardi*, through the troubled "Victorianism" of *Clarel*, to the "modernism" of "Bartleby the Scrivener" and "Pebbles"—with the "American" *Moby-Dick* as a side trip along the way. No one demonstrates better the complex interweaving of British and American writing in the fabric of English literature or the impossibility of tracing out its varied patterns without due attention to both warp and woof.

An additional benefit to be derived from the consideration of American writers in the context of English literature as a whole is the substantial basis it provides for our estimation of a writer's literary importance. To be sure, this reconsideration will have little effect on the reputations of the acknowledged American masters, since it is their contributions to English literature, not their putative "Americanness," that earned them their reputations in the first place. Nevertheless, there are a number of American writers, like Howells, whose reputations rest mainly on their superiority to all but a few of their own countrymen or on their historical importance rather than on their importance to the development of English literature, and whose place in the American pantheon is owing largely to the nationalists's need to flesh out the rather short list of truly important American writers with merely good ones. Compared to S. Weir Mitchell and Harold Frederick, Howells is a very good writer indeed and much more deserving of a spot in any anthology of American Literature. As a figure in nineteenth-century American cultural history, moreover, he is certainly more significant than Melville and perhaps as influential as Stowe. But considered in the context of English literature, alongside writers like Dickens and Hawthorne, his undisputed literary excellences and his impact on American culture count for very little, and his reputation finds its proper level with those of Elizabeth Gaskell and Edmund Gosse.

There are, on the other hand, American writers whose reputations have suffered from these nationalistic associations. When Charles Brockden Brown is removed from the long line of English writers whose works he read and who read his and is placed at the beginning of a purely American line that leads straight through Poe, Hawthorne, and Melville to Faulkner, his work seems merely primitive, a series of necessarily stumbling attempts to make art out of unpromising local materials, in a Philistine society, without literary models. Located where he belongs, however, at a major turning point in the history of English fiction, about halfway between *Robinson Crusoe* and *Heart of Darkness,* he no longer seems a tiller of the thin American soil, starting something that later (and therefore luckier) Americans would finish. He appears, on the contrary, to be examining the epistemological, ontological, and ethical foundations upon which English fiction had been erected in the eighteenth century and to be surveying the new philosophical ground upon which a new house of fiction would be built in the century to come. There are, happily, signs in recent criticism that Brown's literary importance is beginning to be recognized.[36] Although he is still too often portrayed standing alone in Philadelphia, with the trackless forest at his back and West Egg somewhere ahead, as if he were a feature on the American landscape, one occasionally finds his writings compared usefully to those of Rilke, Kafka, and Marquez. Welcome as they are, however, these efforts at reassessment will misfire if in removing Brown from his provincial situation they cause us to forget that he was an American, living in America, writing in English, and working in an established English genre and that this situation played a significant part in determining the nature of his very important contribution to literature in English.

For the literary scholar, perhaps the main virtue of reading American writers in the context of English literature consists in the enriched opportunities that the method offers for the interpretation of individual works. Neither the courtly packaging of John Smith's practical advice and democratic sentiments in the *Generall Historie* nor the antic style of Nathaniel Ward's Simple Cobler make any sense until we see these odd combinations of container and content as expressions of the writer's ambivalent attitudes toward their British audience—as acts of accommodation and aggression at once. The implications of Franklin's inability to decide, finally, whether his success is attributable to Providence or to luck, to foresight or to experience, become apparent only when the *Autobiography* is read in the company of Bunyan and Defoe, its announced progenitors. Hawthorne's fictive examination of marriage as a metaphoric solution to the conflict between natural energy and social or metaphysical forms is not even apparent unless *The Scarlet Letter* is read alongside works like *The Marriage of Heaven and Hell*, *Waverley*, *Prometheus Unbound*, "Lamia," *Jane Eyre*, *In Memoriam*, *Mill on the Floss*, and "Goblin Market," as well as *Arthur Mervyn*, *The Deerslayer*, *Pierre*, *Leaves of Grass*, and *Portrait of a Lady*. Now and again in recent criticism one finds an American work considered, to considerable advantage, as a product or an example of some movement in British literary history: Emerson's essays as Romantic, *Huckleberry Finn* as Victorian, *The Education of Henry Adams* as Edwardian.[37] Preferable though they are to the customary separation of American works from British writings, by employing the conventional categories of British literary history these treatments effectually maintain that separation and so fail to realize many of the interpretive possibilities that arise when American works are construed as English instances, rather than simply as either British or American ones. Hank Morgan's tragedy, like Dombey's, reflects his creator's dismay at what the New World had done to the Old.

On a more theoretical level, the inclusion of American writings in English literature can resolve the old debate between history and criticism that has bedeviled the study of American literature for decades. What determines the most "American" books, the ones we should study and teach—historical importance or literary value? Should we give our attention to works like *Ben Hur,* which almost everyone read and may therefore be presumed to reflect late-nineteenth-century American literary taste, or to Emily Dickinson's poems, which almost no one read until this century, when they began to be assigned in American literature courses by teachers who found them congenial to modern critical tastes? In short, should the past govern the present, as the historians insist, or should the present govern the past, as the critics would have it?[38] The choices are equally unattractive. If historical considerations prevail, we end up studying literarily inferior works; but if our critical tastes are allowed to dictate the canon, we are left with a very distorted picture of the American past.

The difficulty arises entirely from the intrusion of the nonliterary term "American" into what is properly a literary matter, from the confusion of literary history with American history and of literary importance with Americanness. Literary history is the history of literature, not the history of some national culture that is revealed, partly, in its literature. Literary importance, by the same token, is importance to the history of literature, not to the history of the place where the literature was written. The idea of American literature forces us to choose between America and literature, between nonliterary history and ahistorical literature. When the term "American" is expunged, however, literary history and literary criticism come together on their common literary ground, and the conflict between them vanishes. Nor need we fear, as the historians of American literature so often claim, that the removal of American writings from America will leave them adrift in ahistorical, aesthetic space, where literary works from all places and periods are free to revolve about each other endlessly. For, like every literary work, those written in America have a home in their language; and since what we call American literature is written in English, it resides in the English language, which is at once a more literary place than "America" and a more historical one than "literature." Located there, these American writings can be evaluated critically for their importance to the history of literature in English, by literary critics and literary historians working in concert rather than at cross-purposes.

Once American writings are situated where they belong, in English literature—thus avoiding both the historian's error of transgressing the boundaries between languages—the nonliterary conditions of American life can reenter the picture to help explain how a work like *Walden* happened to take the shape that has made it literarily important. It is simply a matter of deciding where our real interests lie. Do we want to be historians, using the techniques of literary analysis, among others, to answer questions about American culture, civilization, and the like? Or do we want to be literary scholars, using historical information, among other sorts, to solve literary problems? Those who choose the historical road cannot content themselves with studying the acknowledged American classics, or American writings in English, or even American writings. They must examine American things of all sorts—commercial products, architecture, transportation, the arts—everything that goes to make up American life. Those who aim to be literary scholars, on the other hand, must take care to construe their materials in literary rather than political, geographical, or historical terms. But no matter which course we choose to pursue, we cannot justifiably go on restricting our studies to a handful of necessarily unique literary works by such obviously atypical Americans as Hawthorne, Melville, and Whitman on the assumption that this unrepresentative collection of masterpieces constitutes a subject in itself or that it will tell us, all by itself, anything very reliable either about America or about literature.

The mistake of American literary study has been, from the very beginning, the idea that an appreciation of American writing depends upon our keeping it separate from the rest of the world, especially Britain. If we study American writers in company with their British contemporaries (except for purposes of drawing very dubious distinctions), we fear, they will lose not only their American identity but the literary virtues we attribute to them. The case is, rather, that this strategy has prevented us from realizing the very substantial claims to literary consequence that can be made on behalf of American writing. When we trumpet the virtues of Emerson, Hawthorne, and Whitman in isolation, the unavoidable intemperance of our judgments fairly begs chastisement from those debunkers who maintain that a comparison of these writers with their European counterparts would forbid such puffery.[39] Considered by itself, American writing of the seventeenth and eighteenth centuries will always seem little more than a literary desert. Separated from the literary world in which they lived and wrote, and lumped together with such literary hacks and clowns as Crockett, Barnum, and Tourgee, even the American masters have the look of gifted roughnecks—"great big somethings," as Swinburne said of Whitman, on the rude outskirts of British literary civilization. Situated where they belong by virtue of their language, however, in the mainstream of English literary history that flows from the Renaissance to the Modern era, the American giants would soon detach themselves from the pygmies to stand alongside their British peers as fellow contributors to the evolution of English literature. By that criterion, who would be the more important English writer—Tennyson or Whitman? Trollope or Melville? Arnold or Dickinson? If the aim of American literary study is to make big claims for American writers, we could hardly find a better, more defensible way to do it.

American Things/Literary Things: The Problem of American Literary History

The appearance of a new compendious history of American literature from Columbia University Press and the promise of still another, from Cambridge, ought to be an occasion for rejoicing among scholars in the field. As the editors of these cooperative projects have more than once reminded us, the need is urgent: nearly four decades of original research into American's literary past lie between us and the last comprehensive survey of the subject, Robert E. Spiller's *Literary History of the United States*. What is more, the Great Theoretical Awakening of recent years has revived from its long New Critical sleep the idea of literary history itself, redefining its aims and devising new methods for its conduct. Nevertheless, an enthusiastic reception for these awaited volumes seems altogether unlikely. Unless they manage somehow to escape the objections that have greeted every exercise in the genre since Samuel Knapp published his *Lectures on American literature, with Remarks on Some Passages of American History,* a century and a half ago, some reviewers will find their interest in American history unliterary, others will find their literary preferences unhistorical, and one may even say what René Wellek said of Spiller's tome back in 1949: that the compilers seem to have no very clear idea of what either literature or history is.[1]

To be sure, such problems are not peculiar to histories of American literature. " 'History' and 'literature'," Howard Mumford Jones once observed, "are terms the meaning of which everybody knows, but the definition of which nobody can give."[2] The inability to define their key terms has sometimes led literary historians into a kind of despair. "The subject of literary history," Wellek complained in 1941, "has been under fire for several decades. . . . Even enthusiasts for the subject do not seem to envisage a future for it." Apparently counting himself among these despondent enthusiasts, Wellek went on to ask "whether it is *possible* to write literary history . . . a history of literature that will be both literary and history." The accumulated evidence did not seem promising: "It must be admitted that most histories of literature are either social histories or histories of thought as mirrored in literature, or a series of impressions and judgments on individual works of art arranged in a more or less chronological order."[3] Not even the decline of formalist criticism and the rise of literary theory in recent years has produced a solution to the basic problem of literary history. In the view of theorists like Claudio Guillén, "To explore the idea of literary history" is still "the main theoretical task that confronts the student of literature"; while to practitioners of the art like Earl Miner, literary history remains "as much a thing to be desired and despaired of as was theoretical criticism not many years ago."[4]

Nevertheless, the problems of writing a history of American literature seem especially forbidding. It is sufficiently difficult, Wellek notes, "to trace the history of a national literature as an art, when the whole framework invites to references essentially unliterary, to speculations about national ethics and national characteristics which have little to do with the art of literature." But "in the case of American literature," Wellek goes on, "where there is no linguistic distinction from another national literature, the difficulties become manifold."[5] Worse yet, for an Americanist, these difficulties are unavoidable. They are, in Howard Mumford Jones's words, "the central issue in the study of American literature,"[6] for the simple reason that the word "American" designates something primarily historical: the United States or the New World or the citizenship of certain writers. Students of French literature can skirt the pitfalls of literary history and still remain students of French literature as long as the texts they study are written in French. But even the most resolutely ahistorical critics of American literature, who have thrown out "history" as a deter-mining factor in the genesis and hence the meaning of literary texts, will find themselves embroiled in history insofar as they re-strict their attention to American writings. Whether we like it or not, the word "American" invokes history, and we can escape the problem of literary history only by giving up the study of Ameri-can literature altogether.

The particular problem of American literary history arises from the fact that while the term "American literature" purports to con-nect to something historical, "America," to something called "lit-erature," these two things are in fact incompatible; for the idea of literature at work here is fundamentally ahistorical, while the sort of history implied by the word "American" is political or geo-graphical rather than literary. As Americanists commonly use the term, "literature" is merely a nominal category for writings that meet their own retroactively imposed criteria of literariness. It does not denote a thing that exists continuously in nature, gives rise to successive literary texts, and thus relates them historically to each other. The word "American," conversely, does not describe some literary feature of the texts it identifies—their language, say, or their style or structure or genre—as would a modifier like "Ro-mantic" or "Russian." It merely denotes the citizenship of their authors, and only by transferring that citizenship from author to text can Americanists even appear to lend the word a literary con-notation. Since Emerson is an American prose writer, it is gener-ally assumed, he must be a writer of American prose. But not even this adjectival switch really succeeds in giving the word "Ameri-can" a literary meaning. If "American prose" means "prose like Emerson's," it obviously excludes most of the prose Americans have written and includes some prose written by non-Americans. If, on the other hand, "American prose" means "prose written by Americans," then the category is too large and far too various to be exemplified by Emerson. In the first case, "American prose" has nothing necessarily to do with America; in the second, "Ameri-can" says nothing of literary significance about the prose.

Because "American literature" posits no necessary relation between the historical entity we call "America" and those writings we call "literature," historians of American literature have had to find some way to fill the intervening space. For purposes of review, the various strategies they have devised may be classified as "historical," "literary," and "mediatory," according to their proponents' relative affection for things American and things literary. Among historical methods, the oldest and the one most clearly predicated by the idea of a national literary history has been to regard literary texts, in the manner of V. L. Parrington, as more or less encoded reflections of American history—whether political, cultural, religious, or intellectual. There are, to be sure, those who believe that the literature of any country has value only in the context of nonliterary history. "If literary studies are divorced from the larger concerns of cultural history," D. W. Robertson has said, "they will eventually wither away."[7] In the study of American literature, however, where nationality, as Wellek noted, is not linguistically definite, nonliterary history has been seen as especially crucial to literary history. Any survey of American literature, Fred Lewis Pattee said, "must be written against the background of American history" if it is even to seem American.[8] A working knowledge of "social, economic, and political history," Norman Foerster maintained, "is peculiarly important in the case of American literature."[9] Harry Hayden Clark agreed that the American literary historian "must keep abreast of his brother students in history and economics."[10] And Louis B. Wright put the case most strenuously of all: "American literature is a part of the infinite complex of American cultural development and must be treated in relation to the rest of cultural phenomena if it is to have any real significance as history."[11]

The main objection to this approach is that, even though the historical decoding of texts may require considerable skill in literary analysis, the treatment is finally unliterary insofar as it locates the ultimate value of literature outside itself, in the so-called real world of ideas and events that literature is supposed to reflect.

Modifying his earlier position somewhat, Foerster objected to the normal procedures of American literary history on the ground that they lead scholars "to view literature as a supplement to history."[12] In doing so, furthermore, they ascribe the character of literary works to extraliterary conditions and thus imply an environmental determinism as rigid and undemonstrable as that proposed by Mme de Staël or Taine. Inevitably, as Wellek has said, the study of literature as a product and a mirror of nonliterary history will crowd out all specifically literary concerns,[13] including the very criteria by which literature is normally distinguished from ordinary writing.

It is this deep suspicion regarding literary values that finally discredits the historical solution to the problem of literary history. When knowledge about America is the prime concern, our ideas about literature cannot be permitted to interfere in the selection of data. "Literary criticism and literary history," Arthur Schlesinger, Sr., once proclaimed, "are two distinct branches of scholarship, each with its own point of view and technique, and having no more in common than, say, history in general and the study of ethics. Until the historian frees himself from the domination of literary critics, his work is certain to fall short of its highest promise."[14] Envisaging a literary history so committed to "historical values" that it would make no distinction between literary and nonliterary writings, Louis Wright proposed that "literature" be construed as "the total output of the printing press."[15] Once the historical method has arrived at this point of critical indifference, of course, it can go a step farther and place a higher value on subliterature. "No historian of American letters," Schlesinger said, "however highly he may personally esteem Ralph Waldo Emerson, could treat the middle third of the nineteenth century without devoting considerably more space to William H. McGuffey."[16] And from there it can take the final step to Pattee's view that inferior literature alone has any historical significance: "To study only the literature of aristocracy is to be ignorant of America, for America, taking all of its elements together, is synonymous with

vulgarity.["17] Granted its premises, the historical method is virtually guaranteed to produce a literary history than is not a history
of literature.

Recent years have seen a modification of the historical approach
that aims to redress the imbalance between history and literature
by abandoning chronological development to concentrate on the
relations between literary and extraliterary events in isolated periods or authorial careers. Earl Miner, for example, has diagnosed
the problem of literary history in general as a dependence on narrative, a rhetorical mode of explanation that was discredited by
the New Critics and will have to be replaced if literary history is
to regain its former authority.[18] But this solution throws out the
baby with the bath. While it is true that the New Critics attacked
narrative history, they did so because the history in question was
unliterary, not because it was narrated. Unless history takes a narrative form, in fact, it can only mean "extraliterary events," the
very thing that formalists sought to exclude from literary studies.
As Tzvetan Todorov has argued, when literary history is stripped
of its diachronic dimension, it ceases to be a history of literature
and becomes simply a misleading name for the sociology or psychology of literature.[19] And whatever else these disciplines may
do for our understanding of literary texts, by fixing literature in
the circumstances of its production they tend to ignore the circumstances of reception, that "use" of texts that determines their
relative literariness, and thus to reinforce the very distinction between literature and "history" that literary history must find some
way to rectify.

The second principal strategy applied to this problem by American literary historians has been to move to the literary side of the
intervening gap and, instead of burying literature in its historical
ground, deal exclusively with the most critically esteemed texts
produced in America, on the assumption that these acknowledged
masterpieces are the best source of information about America.
Like the historical method, this one is susceptible to varying degrees of application. Having first determined, with Harry Clark,
that all literature that falls "considerably below the esthetic par . . .

belongs to the social historian rather than the literary historian," one may follow the advice of Henry Seidel Canby and study the best American literature "as art conditioned by the American environment."[20] Or instead of placing America and literature side by side, the critical historian may adopt a procedure recommended by Clark, setting the literature in front and viewing "the background . . . through the 'windows' of the foreground."[21] Whereas both of these methods presuppose an independent knowledge of the historical background, Lionel Trilling considered America's literary classics an altogether sufficient source—indeed, the only reliable source—of information about American culture.[22] With historical data safely out of the way, the road lies open to a view of American history as a "theme" that the critic discovers in a historically discontinuous series of texts selected entirely on the basis of literary merit. No longer the handmaiden of history, literature has become its mistress.

The critical method, however, raises as many questions as does the historical approach it seeks to supplant. By what logic can the best American writings be considered the most American when the criteria by which these texts are chosen have nothing necessarily to do with degrees of Americanness and when we know as well as Pattee did that, since the American literary norm (like the literary norm everywhere) is decidedly inferior, the best is by definition unrepresentative? How can we be sure, when literature is our sole source of knowledge, that it is American culture and not something less geographically specific that we are seeing when we look at our literary masterworks? "The weakness of literary history in general," Louis Wright complained, "and of American literary history in particular, has been a tendency to interpret presumed masterpieces *in vacuo,* or against an artificial background of the author's own derivation."[23] And it is certainly true that an excessive reliance on presently adjudged masterpieces must give us a distorted picture of their times. Regarding the reduced attention paid to poets like Bryant, Longfellow, and Whittier in successive histories of American literature, William Charvat wrote: "The shrinkage may be justified on critical but hardly on historical grounds, for the importance of these poets in their own century cannot decrease. We err, as historians, in allowing the taste of the modern reader to nullify the taste of the nineteenth-century reader."[24] What permits the critical method to nullify that nineteenth-century taste, of course, is the assumption that this earlier judgment was historically conditioned, while its own is somehow timeless. If the weakness of the historical method was, in Howard Mumford Jones's words, its lack of a "point of view,"[25] the corresponding fault of the critical approach is a point of view so domineering that no fact of American history can withstand its powers of invention.

Like their counterparts in the historical camp, some proponents of the critical method have sought to solve the problem of American literary history by finessing it. Applying Trilling's principles to the canon of great American novels, Richard Chase taught a generation of Americanists how to choose their materials on critical grounds, line them up chronologically, assume that whatever recurs there in the way of theme or imagery or form or style is American, and then regard any variations in this recurring thing as evidence of its historical evolution.[26] That Chase managed to beg both the question of Americanness, by locating it a priori in the texts studied, and the question of historical continuity, by neglecting to explain how the recurring literary feature was transmitted from text to text, did nothing whatsoever to discredit his model among a professoriat committed to the idea of a unique American literary tradition. Indeed, almost no one complained when Chase's followers avoided the questions of Americanness and historical continuity altogether by merely subjecting a succession of American masterpieces to the same sort of critical analysis without saying anything at all about what makes them American or relates them historically to each other. To cite only one example of the hundreds available: Donald B. Stauffer's *A Short History of American Poetry* (1974) is neither short, at 450 pages, nor a history, since it offers no definition of its subject that would enable us to see different poems as episodes in the development of this supposedly continuous entity, nor a study of "American poetry," since it does not explain what makes these particular poems either uniquely or characteristically American—and so ought to have been called "A Long Collection of Critical Essays on Selected Poems in English by Some Well-known American Writers."

Dissatisfaction with the choice between turning literary works into historical documents and turning history into a convenient fiction has led our third class of American literary historians to seek a mediatory position between the divided realms of literature and history. Samuel Knapp located this middle ground between the covers of his own book, which huddled together his "Lectures on American Literature" and his "Passages of American History." Norman Foerster removed it to the mind of the ideal scholar-critic, who evaluates his materials critically even as he treats them historically.[27] Later Americanists, seeking a more perfect union between these warring states, have posited a sort of ideal universe—variously called "mind," "culture," "experience," "dream," "myth," and "ideology"—in which both history and literature may be supposed to coexist. As Leo Marx has said, however, these "large collective mental formations . . . seem unmoored—a ghostly, free-floating cloud of abstractions only distantly related, like the casting of a shadow" to the actual products of human behavior they purport to explain.[28] Because they are purely conceptual, they can attain historical status, a semblance of continuous objective existence, only through reification. And once reified, of course, they can seem to account for, even to cause, the phenomena that generated the conception in the first place. To be sure, these "ambitious schemes," as Warner Berthoff once called them,[29] have produced the most influential studies of American literature to date. Nevertheless, they have merely imagined what they could not discover: some actual common ground on which the divided realms of literature and history might be united.

II

The problem of American literary history has a history of its own, one exactly as long as that of the idea of American literature itself. Toward the end of the eighteenth century, according to

Claudio Guillén, the Renaissance and Enlightenment conception of literature as a timeless whole, grounded in a universal poetics and rhetoric, was shattered by an erupting interest in individuality, which emphasized the differences among writers, and in historical change, which emphasized the differences among literary periods. "The main consequence" of this upheaval, Guillén argues, "was a serial view of literature as a chronological succession of individual works and writers. To counteract this seriality and compensate for the loss of an independent focus found in poetics or poetry itself, literary historians were forced to form new alliances and seek outside means of support. The concept of the nation, regarded by definition as an organic whole, growing and developing in history, became the all-embracing principle of unity."[30]

From this *mariage de convenance* between literature and national history the idea of American literature was born, with the distinctive parental features that it would wear throughout its life already stamped inharmoniously upon its infant visage. When the phrase "American literature" first came into use in the 1780s, it denoted one or the other of two quite different things. While everyone agreed that the term referred to something wanting, rather than to something already present in the world, for some critics the desired object was a body of writings by Americans that could be considered *literature,* whereas for others it was a way of writing that could be considered distinctively *American.* The literary party worried that Americans, removed as they were from the capitals of civilization, might slip into a barbarous vernacular that would sever them permanently from world literature. The Americanists, on the other hand, lamented the dependence of native writers on a European language and European standards of eloquence and encouraged the development of a distinct American idiom, however unlovely it might sound to European ears.[31]

From the very beginning, then, "literature" suggested something un-American, while "American" implied something unliterary. To Edward W. Johnson, the advocates of a distinctive American literature seemed not to know what "a literature" is. To Edward Tyrell Channing, on the other hand, any American writer whose work resembled that of any foreigner was a virtual traitor. Grenville Mellen opined that "an American work of taste *cannot* differ from an English" work of equal literary merit. Channing disagreed: the value of American literature lies in its "nativeness.... No matter for rudeness, ... it is enough that all is our own." For Longfellow, "every book written by a citizen of a country belongs to its national literature." But for Bryant, "it is only the production of genius, taste, and diligence that can find favor at the bar of criticism.... [One's] writings are not to be applauded merely because they are written by an American, and are not decidedly bad." "By a national literature," Cooper said, "we ... mean ... a literature which foreigners may admire, but none can feel, in the deep sanctuary of the heart, but a native." On the contrary, thought Orestes Brownson, the literature of any nation, to deserve the name, "must be addressed to the common understanding and common sentiments of all cultivated readers" throughout the civilized world.[32]

After the Civil War, the debate over the relative importance of literariness and Americanness removed itself from the editorial offices of such journals as the "Universalist" *Knickerbocker Magazine* and the "Nationalist" *Arcturus* to the English departments of those progressive American universities where the study of "modern" literature, including a course or two in American writers, was beginning to infiltrate the classical and philological curriculum. Situated in these scholarly precincts, the controversy shifted its attention from what American literature should be to what it had been. The points in dispute, however, remained essentially unchanged: did American literature comprise all identifiably American writings, no matter how unliterary, or only the very best writings by American authors? And the solutions to this persistent problem offered by the scores of American literary histories that poured from the academic presses over the seven decades between John S. Hart's *Manual of American Literature* (1873) and *The Lit-*

erary History of the United States (1948) were equally predictable. Charles F. Richardson's pioneering *American Literature* (1887) made history and literature separate but equal, devoting one of its two volumes to "The Development of American Thought" and the other to "American Poetry and Fiction." W. B. Otis's *American Verse, 1625–1807* (1909) stood on the historical foot, including in its pages "all important American verse . . . which is worthy of note because of its connection with American history." Henry Beers moved closer to the literary pole in saying that his *Outline Sketch of American Literature* (1887), "though meant to be mainly a history of American *belles-lettres* . . . makes some mention of historical and political writings." Going about as far in the literary direction as the genre allowed, E. C. Stedman selected for his *Poets of America* (1885) figures whose work evinced the rise of "American song" and "the national sentiment," rather than the development of its "riches, knowledge, and power." Three years later, Stedman's collaborator in the *Library of American Literature,* Ellen Hutchinson, drew him back to a position of perfect equilibrium by choosing for that project works said to be at once the most "select and characteristic," "the best" and "most representative" of "the different stages of American history."[33]

With the advent of the New Criticism after World War II and its interdict upon extraliterary criteria in the identification and evaluation of literary texts, the golden age of American literary history came to a close. For the next twenty years or so, only histories derived entirely from demonstrable masterpieces could expect a welcome from literary studies. Even then, the merest shadow of extrinsicality cast by the word "American" in a book title or by the author's predilection for the literature of a single country might evoke from the relentlessly stateless critics anathemas as shrill as any heard from the old Knickerbocker group.[34] As for those scholars who retained an interest in American things and wanted to study more than the handful of American texts considered worthy to be called literature, their only safety lay in the neutral territory of American studies, between the warring camps of historical scholarship and literary criticism, where neither historical facts nor aesthetic discriminations were either forbidden or too much insisted upon. Here one might proceed either from an idea of America to its manifestation in the works of printers, steamboat pilots, carpenters, sailors, preachers, slaves, and other nonwriters, or from an idea of literature as the artistic expression of profoundest truth to a picture of the American past that the past itself would have hardly recognized, without much fear of rousing either the critical or the scholarly watchdogs. The problem of American literary history, however, remained unsolved. "Useful as . . . the American Studies programs in our Universities" may be, Jay B. Hubbell felt obliged to conclude, they "have not taught us how to synthesize aesthetic criticism with literary and cultural history." [35]

While American studies were running in place on the middle ground between aesthetic criticism and historical scholarship, the opposing camps, weary of stalemate, began to shift their positions to higher theoretical terrain. "Historical" studies cast off the positivist assumptions and scientific pretensions that had brought them into discredit, reformulating their ideas of literature, on the one hand, and of society, politics, or psychology, on the other, in terms of structural principles supposedly common to all forms of human behavior. Viewed from this height, "history" lost its ontological primacy and explanatory power and became itself a thing to be explained. Not to be left behind in the revolution, criticism began a campaign of theoretical terrorism against the assumptions entertained by literary formalism and historical scholarship alike regarding the authority of texts, the validity of interpretation, the mechanics of referentiality, the ontological status of "writers," "works," and "readers," and the very existence of what is called "the past." The result of these concerted movements toward a radical skepticism regarding all forms of historical and literary judgment has been to unite "literature" and "history" more closely than at any time perhaps since the breakup of the Christian cosmos and the consequent divorce of "poetic" from "scientific" knowledge. The modern terms of agreement, however, are so clearly inimical to normative definitions of "literature," to organic models of nationhood, and to diachronic patterns of historical development as to discredit the very idea of an American literary history. And it must be said that recent work in the field makes very little headway against these theoretical impediments. *Toward a New American Literary History,* a festschrift for Arlin Turner published in 1980,[36] opens with the editors' announcement that the included essays bespeak the need for a new departure and point the requisite direction; but the essays themselves inspire no conviction that the long desire for an American literary history is about to be satisfied. Some of them trace a history, some deal with literature, and some refer to all or part of America. But none of them does all of these things at once, and the collection as a whole offers no clear indication of how the ideas of history, literature, and America might be synthesized.

After a very long run, it appears that American literary history is right where it started: forced to choose between literarily insignificant ephemera and the necessarily unrepresentative productions of literary genius, obliged to fudge its definition of either literature or of Americanness, and fated ultimately to reinforce the very impression that the institution of American literature was created to rectify—the impression that America and literature have nothing to do with each other. We have American things, and we have literary things; but we have nothing typically American that can be called literary and nothing literary that can be called uniquely or characteristically American. Because these two things won't go together, the only possible history of "American literature," it seems, would be a survey of all uses to which this evocative but finally empty phrase has been put since it first entered the language two hundred years ago.

III

Unsatisfactory as the existing models of American literary history may be, they enable us to identify the requirements for a more workable scheme, "to elaborate," as Wellek demanded, "a new ideal of literary history and new methods which would make its realization possible."[37] First of all, our ideal literary history must be a *history,* which is to say not just a portrait of some isolated past event or a chronology of essentially discrete events but an account of changes that have occurred over time in some identifiable, continuously existing thing. Second, this history must deal primarily with *literature,* not with some other human activity—politics, thought, society, or whatever—that is merely reflected in literature and not with writing that can be called literature only by confounding the two terms. And third, it must close the gap between history and literature not by treating literature as an archive of historical documents in stylish dress or by abstracting a history from literature but by placing history and literature on a common ground, one that has its own historical existence, independent of its manifestations in literature, and is at the same time essential to literature. Could we discover this common ground, we could define "literature" and "history" in terms of each other, rather than in mutual opposition, and thus erect upon it a literary *history* that would also be a history of *literature.*[38]

But what is this historically continuous ground to be? It cannot be literature itself, as some comparatists have proposed,[39] since "literature" is merely a name given to different writings at different times to denote certain attitudes toward them or the uses to be made of them. Nor can literary history be founded upon the "values" or "norms" by which literature is distinguished from ordinary writing, for these standards too are historically discontinuous, "so that what appeared to be 'universal art' in 1920," as D. W. Robertson has said, "must now be made 'universal' on quite other grounds."[40] Neither will genres, literary forms, provide a basis for literary history.[41] Like "literature," these categories are abstracted from the very works upon which they are imposed and consequently vary with the works selected for analysis. Literary referents, similarly—subjects, themes, ideas—have no historical existence apart from the texts in which they appear and are in any case not essential to literature.[42] And while literary reception is certainly an essential aspect of literature, it too is historically discontinuous, a collection of discrete historical events that can be connected to each other only upon some equally ineffable ground, such as "consciousness" or "audience."[43]

So far as I know, the only thing that meets all of the desiderata for a ground of literary history is language. First of all, on the level of what linguists calls "competence," languages exist continuously, in the same fundamental form over long periods of time, permitting anyone who possesses the necessary competence to read any text that employs them, no matter when, where, or in what style that text was written. Second, languages also change, on the level called "performance," allowing us to regard texts written at different times in different styles as variations upon the same unchanging competence.[44] Third, unlike such purely conceptual categories as "literature" or "the novel," which are derived from very dissimilar texts after the fact and then imposed upon those texts in order to lend them an air of identity, languages exist prior to, and independent of, the texts in which we find them.[45] And finally, unlike subjects, themes, and ideas, language is essential to literature. Every literary text arises from a language, has its very being in that language, remains dependent for its meaning upon the survival of that language, and is related historically to every other literary text in the same language by their common, identifying grammar.

It may even be that what actually distinguishes what we call literature from other sorts of writing is our recognition of its peculiar relation to language. While every piece of writing is conditioned by the basic grammar and the performative history of the language in which it is written, languages are also conditioned, more or less, by every textual performance in those languages. According to this measure, "literature" may simply be the name we give to those texts that appear to have conditioned their respective languages the most, creating new lexical, semantic and syntactic possibilities for all subsequent writings in that language and hence new parameters for the interpretation of all previous ones.[46] When literature is defined linguistically, as the most apparently consequential events in the development of any written language, literary texts take on a historical dimension without our having to think of them as aesthetic reflections of extraliterary circumstances. And when history is defined in the same linguistic terms, as a sequence of changes effected in a language by literary texts, it can be thought of as a literary product that is not simply a convenient fiction. Removed from their separate domains in ahistorical literature and extraliterary history and brought together on the common ground of language, which is both historical in its own right and essential to literature, literature and history can be defined in common terms that permit a truly literary history, a record of the evolving dialogue between written texts and their respective languages.[47]

A word of explanation is necessary at this point. In proposing a literary history based on language, I do not mean by "language" some metalinguistic concept or a loose metaphor for behavior in general. I mean the actual language, the "tongue" in which a particular literature is written. Since the two necessary conditions for any history—continuous identity and change—are met in the case of literary history by grammatical competence and written performance, and since languages differ on the level of competence, a literary history cannot deal with texts in more than one language without slipping its historical mooring. We can have a history of Russian literature or French literature or German literature. But until someone manages to formulate the universal competence that underlies all languages, we cannot realize the comparatists' dream of "a universal literary history . . . cutting across all linguistic barriers."[48] Nor will the structuralists' concept of language permit such a history. That concept has more to do with a system of structures common to writing and nonwriting than with an actual grammar shared by all languages, and, as Earl Miner has said, its main weakness lies in its failure to take "account of the striking differences among languages."[49] On the contrary,

language has proved a workable basis for literary history precisely
to the degree that its practitioners have respected these differences
among languages and confined their attention to performative developments within a single competence.[50]

What makes specific languages uniquely adequate to the requirements of literary history is their temporal duration, their
continuing existence over time. But tongues have another dimension that is equally crucial to literary history: they are also extended geographically. The common language that connects *The
Canterbury Tales* to *The Waste Land* across the centuries also con-
joins *The House of the Seven Gables* and *Bleak House* across the seas.
The literary historian in search of writings that have markedly
altered their language must regard these two dimensions of the
linguistic ground—chronology and geography—as inseparable.
For just as a literary event can occur at any *time* in the history of a
language, such an event can occur in any *place* where that language
is being written. Any subdivision of a linguistic geography along,
say, political or physical lines, therefore, is apt to obscure the history of that language no less than would a decision to sever its
temporal line at some arbitrary point. Insofar as our ability to
construct a literary history that is both literary and historical depends upon our keeping in view all of the times and all of the
places where significant literary developments in a language may
have occurred, we must avoid any temptation to interfere with its
chronological and geographical integrity.

IV

Returning by way of this theoretical detour to the problem of
American literary history, we may now see more clearly why that
project, for all of its nods to history on the one side and to literature on the other, has never managed to integrate these two essential components of literary history. Because the word "American"
does not designate a language, American literature provides no
linguistic ground upon which that integration might occur. On
the contrary, Americans have written in many languages, all of

which (with the exception of the indigenous tongues) transcend the political and physical boundaries of America and form distinct linguistic worlds, each with its own history and geography. Even if we restrict the domain of American literature to writings in English, as is customary, that language, not America, is the ground on which its history must be constructed.

This ground cannot be subdivided temporally at some point in American history; as Cooper observed in 1828, "The authors [previous] to the revolution are common property, and it is quite idle to say that an American has not just as good a right to claim Milton, and Shakespeare, and all the old masters of the language, for his countrymen, as an Englishman."[51] Nor can the anglophone world be divided geographically or politically, for the simple reason that British and American English have not developed independently. Printed texts have always circulated far too freely back and forth across the Atlantic for either region to remain untouched by linguistic changes originating abroad.[52] This world cannot even be broken up into separate cultures. Considered geographically, cultures are linguistic entities; "language," in Roger Fowler's words, "interpenetrates with culture." Considered historically, cultures develop in concert with language; periods of deep cultural change, D. W. Robertson has noticed, tend to "coincide with periods of linguistic change . . . described by historical linguists." As for the function of literature in this equation, Seymour Katz points out that "literature plays a central role in the development of a language [, which] is to say that it plays a central role in the development of a culture."[53]

The history of what we call American literature, in short, is inseparable from the history of literature in English as a whole. To be sure, Americanists normally resist any such conflation of British and American writings on their common linguistic ground, for fear that, removed from American history and thrown into competition with British masterpieces, American literature would lose its Americanness and its literariness at once. And so it would, to the extent that the American anthology, like its British counterpart, is padded out with writings whose nationality is merely authorial or referential and whose literariness is merely generic or gustatory. A deserving few of our national treasures, however, would survive this translation with their Americanness and their literariness not only intact but clarified and, for once, reconciled. We did not canonize Emerson's essays, *Walden, Moby-Dick, Leaves of Grass, Huckleberry Finn,* and Emily Dickinson's poems because they seemed to conform more closely to some universal idea of literature than "Thanatopsis" and *Gates Ajar* or because they reflect American history more clearly than *Uncle Tom's Cabin* or "Old Ironsides." We call them literature because they seem to speak—indeed, to have invented—the language that constitutes our modern world. And they seem to us American because the world of modern English is itself so much an American creation— the product of changes undergone by the language over the centuries since the discovery, both in its efforts to comprehend the historically unfolding world that was born with the discovery and as a result of its transportation to the New World.[54]

The present canon of American literary masterworks, we should remember, first came into view in the light of this modern "Americanized" English, as radiated from the work of British, American, and Irish expatriates after World War I. Until the modernists taught American readers to hear in the unsettling rhythms of Thoreau, Whitman, and Mark Twain, rather than in the limpid sonorities of Irving, Bryant, and Longfellow, the clearest pre-echoes of their own modern idiom, such experiments in English style could hardly be thought of as "literature." With the dawning awareness of this new linguistic present, however, there emerged, in keeping with T. S. Eliot's historical model, the outlines of a new literary past, an international "modern tradition" that would explain, as neither Arnold's timeless aestheticism nor Howells's rising realism could, the unexpected convergence of Britain's and America's supposedly divergent literary histories in stateless modernism.

Unfortunately, Anglo-American criticism would decline to bring this new tradition fully into view. Although modernism altered both British and American literary history along very similar lines and even caused everything written in English after 1918 or so to be routinely combined under the rubric of the "Modern" period, the net effect of this Modernist revisioning, quite ironically, was that complete nationalist compartmentalization of all earlier English writings that we take for granted today. By conferring unwonted literary status upon America's most idiosyncratic stylists, it seems, the modern tradition provided what America had been looking for ever since the Revolution, a corpus of patently non-British masterpieces that could be arranged to create a national literary history. Whereas the emergence of international English modernism had demanded an international literary history, going all the way back to the discovery and tracing the increasing presence of America in the language and of the language in America, the histories of British and American literature would keep to their separate paths, tracing supposedly independent national traditions that, purposely ignoring the historical geography of the language that produced English modernism, have never managed to explain very clearly where we are or how we got here.

To answer these questions, the modern literary historian must remove British and American writings from the unliterary precincts of national history and from ahistorical definitions of literature and restore them to the world from which they arose and to which they remain inextricably bound: the world of the English language, which is at once a more historical place than any Platonic idea of literature and a more literary place than either Britain or America. Then, taking up a secure position in the present—which is, after all, the thing that history was invented to explain—the literary historian must identify those texts, both British and American, that appear to have contributed most significantly to the construction of the modern English-speaking world, those that the present linguistic situation denominates its "authors." Any text that meets this criterion can be considered literature, whatever its genre, original intention, past reputation, or degree of apparent loveliness. Those that cannot pass this test have no place in the history of literature per se, even though they may have once been considered literature because they conformed to the definition of literature then in force. At the moment when the evolution of the language leaves such writings behind, as it were, they leave the history of literature and become documents in the history of ideas about literature. Nor can we assume that those texts which the present condition of the language identifies as literature will remain so, fixed forever in the evolutionary pattern we discern. Because the shape of the past is conditioned by the present from which it is viewed and toward which it leads, future changes in the language will require their own literary histories.[56] The one we construct today will meet tomorrow's needs for a usable past no better perhaps than yesterday's nationalist literary histories serve ours.

It is difficult to say exactly what this modern history of English literature would look like (should some professor of English ever know our professed subject well enough to write such a book)— which of the big national reputations it might prove historically inconsequential and therefore unworthy of inclusion, which reputedly minor texts it might move into positions of historical and therefore literary prominence, which texts now unknown to literary history because they fall outside the presently approved genres it might bring into the literary fold by demonstrating their importance to the evolution of modern written English. One thing we can say for sure: this modern revision of the literary past would not satisfy America's long-deferred desire for a literary history of its very own. It would, however, satisfy all of the seemingly irreconcilable demands that our nationalist literary historians have regularly made upon each other: Charvat's demand for historical accuracy, "Canby's call for critical discrimination, Spiller's insistence upon breadth, and [Van Wyck] Brooks's appeal for an approach to the past which will have contemporary relevance."[57] Furthermore, by recognizing the essential role of America in the creation of the modern linguistic world from which all of our critical and historical judgments are made, it would discover in American writings a literary and historical significance far greater than anything nationalism has ever imagined. Most important of all, by recognizing that neither this historical past nor the critical present affords an unconditioned ground of literary judgment, that produced work and received text are mutually conditioning aspects of the endlessly evolving historical reality we call literature, this modern history would be "American" in the most essential sense of that word; for it would finally abandon the antique European notion of the modern world as divided geographically into two distinct regions—one New, the other Old—and realize at last that the European discovery of America began the long dialectical process of modern history by which the Old World transformed itself, whether for good or ill, into the New.

Notes

The Earliest American Novel (pp. 45–76)

1. Howard Mumford Jones, *The Theory of American Literature,* 2d ed. (Ithaca, N.Y.: Cornell Univ. Press, 1965; repr. 1966), 25. This grandfather clause has its source in nationalist historiography, where colonial America is portrayed as the "seed-bed of the Republic." For a less typological conception of the subject, we must turn to the old imperial historians and their modern progeny. See, for example, Max Savelle and Darold D. Wax, *A History of Colonial America,* 3d ed. (Hinsdale, Ill.: Dryden, 1973).

2. D. H. Dickason, ed. *Mr. Penrose: The Journal of Penrose, Seaman, By William Williams, 1727–91* (Bloomington, Ind. and London: Indiana Univ. Press, 1969), 25–27.

3. J. A. Leo Lemay, *Men of Letters in Colonial America* (Knoxville, Tenn.: Univ. of Tennessee Press, 1972), 138.

4. For information that would permit an accurate plotting of Behn's location on the map of ideas about the Golden Age, see her poem of that name (6:138–44) and Harry Levin, *The Myth of the Golden Age in the Renaissance* (Bloomington, Ind.: Univ. of Indiana Press, 1969).

5. *The Works of Aphra Behn,* ed. Montague Summers (London: William Heinemann, 1915), 5:129. Subsequent references to this edition appear in parentheses in the text.

6. For detailed studies of the Brief True Relation, see Jarvis M. Morse, *American Beginnings* (Washington, D.C.: Public Affairs Press, 1952), ch. 2; and Wayne Franklin, *Discoverers, Explorers, Settlers* (Chicago and London: Univ. of Chicago Press, 1979). Differences between this form and that of the romance are outlined in W. C. Spengemann, *The Adventurous Muse* (New Haven, Conn.: Yale Univ. Press, 1977), chs. 1 and 2.

7. Richard Hakluyt, *Voyages* (London: J. M. Dent and Sons, 1907), 1:19; and John Smith, *Works,* ed. Edward Arber and A. G. Bradley (Edinburgh: J. Grant, 1910), 2:625.

8. For a full discussion of these cultural epiphanies in voyage narratives and their impact on literature, see Stephen Greenblatt, *Renaissance Self-Fashioning: From More to Shakespeare* (Chicago: Univ. of Chicago Press, 1980), 222–29.

9. See, for example, George Guffey, "Aphra Behn's *Oroonoko:* Occasion and Accomplishment," in *Two English Novelists,* by George Guffey and Andrew Wright (Los Angeles: William Andrews Clark Memorial Library, 1975), 3–41, esp. 37; and Angeline Goreau, *Reconstructing Aphra* (New York: The Dial Press, 1980), 288–89. Although published years

later, we note, Goreau's biography does not confront Guffey's arguments against the idea of Behn's radicalism.

10. Quoted in Goreau, 290.

11. Behn explicitly identifies Charles II with Christ in her *Pindaric on the Death of Our Late Sovereign* (1685) and her *Poem Humbly Dedicated to the Pattern of Piety and Virtue Catherine Queen Dowager* (1685). Charles, Caesar, and Christ, of course, are symbolically akin in having all been kings betrayed by their "sons"—Monmouth, Brutus, and mankind.

12. The controversy regarding Behn's "truthfulness" is surveyed in Goreau, 42–45, and in Frederick M. Link, *Aphra Behn* (New York: Twayne Publishers, 1968), 19–20.

13. Two excellent studies of America's impact on the language are Stephen Greenblatt, "Learning to Curse: Aspects of Linguistic Colonialism in the Sixteenth Century," in *The First Images of America,* ed. Fredi Chiapelli, 2 vols. (Berkeley and Los Angeles, 1976), 1:151–80; and Peter Hulme, "Hurricanes in the Caribbees: The Constitution of the Discourse of English Colonialism," in *1642: Literature and Power in the Seventeenth Century,* ed. Francis Barker et al. (Colchester, England: Univ. of Essex, 1981), 55–83.

14. *Royal Commentaries of the Incas,* trans. H. V. Livermore. 2 vols. (Austin, Tex.: Univ. of Texas Press, 1966), 1:9.

15. John Mason, *Brief History of the Pequot War* (Boston: Kneeland & Green, 1736; repr. in *Massachusetts Historical Society, Collections*), 8:127.

16. In regard to this topic, see Nicholas P. Canny, "The Permissive Frontier: The Problem of Social Control in English Settlements in Ireland and Virginia, 1550–1650," in *The Westward Enterprise,* ed. K. R. Andrews et al. (Detroit: Wayne State Univ. Press, 1978), 17–44. For her play *The Widow Ranter* (1688?), her only other work set in America, Behn apparently used a pamphlet entitled *Strange News from Virginia; Being a Faithful Account of the Life and Death of Nathaniel Bacon, Esquire . . .* (1677), a Brief True Relation of Bacon's rebellion.

17. Paul Delaney, *British Autobiography in the Seventeenth Century* (New York: Columbia Univ. Press, 1969), 173.

18. William Wood, *New England's Prospect* (London: T. Cotes, 1634), n.p.

19. An early approach to this judgment is taken in Rowland M. Hill, "Aphra Behn's Use of Setting," *Modern Language Quarterly* 7 (1946): 189–203.

20. For a counterargument, see F. M. Link, *Aphra Behn,* 142; and for an elaboration of my own, see *The Adventurous Muse,* 245–46.

21. Royall Tyler, *The Algerine Captive,* ed. Don L. Cook (New Haven, Conn.: College and University Press, 1970), 127. For an account of Tyler's "difficulties," see *The Adventurous Muse,* 119–38.

22. The critical reputation of *Oroonoko* is surveyed in Ruthe T. Sheffey, "The Literary Reputation of Aphra Behn" (Ph.D. diss., Univ. of Pennsylvania, 1969).

23. Hans Baron, "The *Querelle* of the Ancients and Moderns as a Problem for Renaissance Scholarship," *Journal of the History of Ideas* 29 (1959): 3–22.

24. John H. Elliot, *The Old World and the New, 1492–1650* (Cambridge: Cambridge Univ. Press, 1970), ch. 2. See also Hugh Honour, *The European Vision of America* (Cleveland, Ohio: The Cleveland Museum of Art, 1975), *passim*.

25. For an excellent discussion of Behn's idea of masculine and feminine "spheres," see Goreau, ch. 4. For an analysis of the impact of the discovery upon ideas of nature and culture, see Clarence Glacken, *Traces on the Rhodian Shore* (Berkeley and Los Angeles: Univ. of California Press, 1967), 354–74.

26. These two passages are quoted in Guffey, 13, 36.

Three Blind Men and an Elephant (pp. 77–97)

1. *De Descriptione Temporum: An Inaugural Lecture* (Cambridge: Cambridge Univ. Press, 1954), 4. Lewis's witty and sensible exposition of the perils of literary periodization can be read with profit as a prologue to the argument of this essay.

2. A. O. Lovejoy, "On the Discrimination of Romanticisms," *PMLA* 39 (1924): 229–53. The long-standing dispute over the meaning of the word is surveyed by Frank Jordan, Jr., in *The English Romantic Poets: A Review of Research and Criticism,* 3d rev. ed. (New York: The Modern Language Association, 1971), 49–53.

3. The meaning of the word "Victorian" is questioned by Norman Friedman, "From Victorian to Modern: A Sketch for a Critical Reappraisal," *Victorian Newsletter* 32 (1967): 20–28; Morse Peckham, "Can 'Victorian' Have a Useful Meaning?" *Victorian Studies* 10 (1967): 273–77; and E. D. H. Johnson, "Romantic, Victorian, and Edwardian," *Princeton University Library Chronicle* 38 (1977): 198–224. Among the many books that treat the continuity of romanticism and modernism, some of the more notable follow: Jacques Barzun, *Romanticism and the Modern Ego* (New York: Little, Brown, 1943; rev. as *Classic, Romantic, and Modern,* 1961); Graham Hough, *The Last Romantics* (London: Duckworth, 1949); Robert Langbaum, *The Poetry of Experience* (New York: Random House, 1957); Frank Kermode, *Romantic Image* (London: Routledge & Kegan Paul, 1957); John Bayley, *The Romantic Survival* (London: Constable, 1957); David Perkins, *The Quest for Permanence* (Cambridge, Mass.: Harvard Univ. Press, 1959); and Charles Schug, *The Romantic Genesis of the Modern Novel* (Pittsburgh, Pa.: Univ. of Pittsburgh Press, 1979).

4. See, for example, Meyer H. Abrams, *Natural Supernaturalism* (New York: Norton, 1971), 427–31.

5. See, for example, Michael Timko, "The Victorianism of Victorian Literature," *New Literary History* 6 (1975): 607–27.

6. See, for example, Morse Peckham, "The Problem of the Nineteenth

Century," in his *The Triumph of Romanticism: Collected Essays* (Columbia, S.C.: Univ. of South Carolina Press, 1970), 87–104; and *Beyond the Tragic Vision* (New York: G. Braziller, 1962).

7. For an account of how the subject came to be defined this way, see Howard Mumford Jones, *The Theory of American Literature* (Ithaca, N.Y.: Cornell Univ. Press, 1948; rev. 1965); and Richard Ruland, *The Rediscovery of American Literature* (Cambridge, Mass.: Harvard Univ. Press, 1967). The premises and methods of American literary scholarship are examined in Warner Berthoff, "Ambitious Scheme," *Commentary* 44 (1967): 110–14; John O. McCormick, "Notes on a Comparative American Literary History," *Comparative Literature Studies* 5 (1968): 167–79; and Michael Colacurcio, "Does American Literature Have a History?" *Early American Literature* 13 (1978): 110–31.

8. Studies that consider both British and American writings fall into several categories: those that examine the American reception and use of British writings—e.g., William Charvat, *The Origins of American Critical Thought, 1810–1835* (Philadelphia: Univ. of Pennsylvania Press, 1936); those that treat the British response to American writings—e.g., Clarence Gohdes, *American Literature in Nineteenth-Century England* (Carbondale, Ill.: Southern Illinois Univ. Press, 1944); those that contrast British and American literature—e.g., Nicolaus Mills, *American and English Fiction in the Nineteenth Century* (Bloomington, Ind.: Indiana Univ. Press, 1973); those that use both British and American works without regard to their nationality—e.g., Edwin M. Eigner, *The Metaphysical Novel in England and America* (Berkeley and Los Angeles: Univ. of California Press, 1978); and those that study the interrelations of British and American writings—e.g., Stephen Spender, *Love-Hate Relations* (New York: Random House, 1974). Marcus Cunliffe attacks the provincial isolationism of both British and American literary studies and calls for cultural studies of "the Atlantic community" in his essay "Americanness," *Southern Review* 4 (1968): 1093–98.

9. John M. Ellis, *The Theory of Literary Criticism: A Logical Analysis* (Berkeley and Los Angeles: Univ. of California Press, 1974).

10. For a model study of this sort, see René Wellek's semantic history of the word "Romantic" in "The Concept of Romanticism in Literary History," in *Concepts of Criticism* (New Haven, Conn.: Yale University Press, 1963), 130ff.

11. Various rationales and methods of literary periodization are outlined in René Wellek and Austin Warren, *Theory of Literature,* 2d ed. (New York: Harcourt, Brace & Co., 1956), 252ff.

12. Melville caught the spirit of his age when, looking back on the Revolutionary period across the tumultuous intervening century, he said that those years "involved a crisis for Christendom not exceeded in its undetermined momentousness at the time by any other era whereof there is record" [*Billy Budd,* ed. Milton R. Stern (Indianapolis: Bobbs-Merrill,

1975), 97]. Meyer Abrams discusses the literary impact of the French Revolution in "English Romanticism: The Spirit of the Age," in *Romanticism Reconsidered,* ed. Northrop Frye (New York: Columbia Univ. Press, 1963), 26–72.

13. The literary impact of World War I is examined in V. de Sola Pinto, *Crisis in English Poetry* (London: Hutchinson's University Library, 1951); C. K. Stead, *The New Poetic* (London: Hutchinson's University Library, 1964), esp. ch. 4; John H. Johnston, *English Poetry of the First World War* (Princeton, N.J.: Princeton Univ. Press, 1964); Bernard Bergonzi, *Heroes' Twilight: A Study of the Literature of the Great War* (New York: Coward-McCann, 1965), Arthur E. Lane, *An Adequate Response* (Detroit: Wayne State Univ. Press, 1972); and Paul Fussell, *The Great War and Modern Memory* (London: Oxford Univ. Press, 1975).

14. The return of American literature to the international scene is documented in *The American Writer and the European Tradition,* ed. Margaret Denny and William H. Gillman (Minneapolis, Minn.: Univ. of Minnesota Press, 1950).

15. René Wellek demonstrates the necessity of combining British and American literature in the conduct of comparative studies, in *Confrontations: Studies in the Intellectual and Literary Relations Between Germany, England, and the United States in the Nineteenth Century* (Princeton, N.J.: Princeton Univ. Press, 1965).

16. My reader will quickly recognize these polar terms. They correspond roughly to Fritz Strich's distinction between the "classical" idea of eternal perfection and the "romantic" idea of infinite movement, as developed in his *Deutsche Klassik und Romantik: Oder Vollendung und Unendlicheit* (Munich: C. H. Beck, 1928). Similar terms have often been applied to the study of nineteenth-century thought and literature; for example, in R. G. Collingwood, *The Idea of Nature* (Oxford: The Clarendon Press, 1943); Bernard Blackstone, *The Lost Travellers* (London: Longmans, 1962); Mark Roberts, *The Tradition of Romantic Morality* (New York: Barnes & Noble, 1973); and Gerald L. Bruns, "The Formal Nature of Victorian Thinking," *PMLA* 90 (1975): 904–18. What distinguishes my use of these terms from their deployment in the works just cited is that those studies tend to associate the two terms with different periods (neoclassic and Romantic, the eighteenth century and the nineteenth, the Enlightenment and the Modern era, Romantic and Victorian) or different places (Britain and America), whereas this essay places both terms together, in a debate that goes on throughout the nineteenth century, throughout the English-speaking world. For an application of a bipolar model to all of nineteenth-century British literature, see Carl Woodring, "Nature and Art in the Nineteenth Century," *PMLA* 92 (1977): 193–202. And for a discussion of the British novel in terms roughly analogous to mine, see Arnold Kettle, *An Introduction to the English Novel* (London and New York: Hutchinson's University Library, 1957).

17. Although the urgency of the debate has waned steadily ever since the modernists agreed, however begrudgingly, to make do with what Frost called a "diminished thing," the debate itself persists in modern criticism about the nineteenth century—for example, in the disagreement between Northrop Frye and Morse Peckham concerning Blake's place in the period. While both see Blake primarily as an advocate of form, rather than of energy, in Frye's view that advocacy places him at the head of the nineteenth century, while for Peckham it places him at the tail end of the Enlightenment. See, for example, Frye's essay "The Keys to the Gates" in *Some British Romantics: A Collection of Essays,* ed. James V. Logan (Columbus, Ohio: Ohio State Univ. Press, 1966), 3–40; and Peckham's *The Triumph of Romanticism* (Columbia, S.C.: Univ. of South Carolina Press, 1970), 213–14.

18. Once again, I do not wish to suggest that the Romantics constitute a party of energy and the Victorians a party of form. On the contrary, such equations seem to me grossly misleading insofar as they make the principle of energy dominant in the early part of the century and the principle of form dominant later, whereas the development appears to proceed in just the opposite direction.

19. For a very different view of the Victorian counterculture and its emergence in the twentieth century, see Morse Peckham, "Victorian Counter-culture," *Victorian Studies* 18 (1975): 257–76.

20. For a study of the subject that inadvertently supports my contention regarding the paucity of these materials, see W. V. Harris, *British Short Fiction in the Nineteenth Century* (Detroit: Wayne State Univ. Press, 1979).

21. For a start on this large subject, see Norman A. Anderson "Rappaccini's Daughter': A Keatsian Analogue?" *PMLA* 83 (1968): 271–83.

22. Virginia Woolf, "Mr. Bennett and Mrs. Brown," in *Collected Essays,* 1 (London: The Hogarth Press, 1966): 319–37.

23. Richard Chase, *The American Novel and Its Tradition* (Garden City, N.Y.: Doubleday and Co., 1957); and D. H. Lawrence, *Studies in Classic American Literature* (New York: T. Seltzer, 1923).

American Writers and English Literature (pp. 115–142)

1. "Essays on American Language and Literature," *North American Review* 1 (1815): 310.

2. Howard Mumford Jones, *The Theory of American Literature,* 2d ed. (Ithaca, N.Y.: Cornell Univ. Press, 1965; repr. 1966), 25.

3. Jones, 25, 29.

4. Of the two statements by Webster, the first is quoted in Benjamin T. Spencer, *The Quest for Nationality* (Syracuse, N.Y.: Syracuse Univ. Press, 1957), 27; the second is from Webster's *Dissertations on the English Language . . .* (Boston: Isaiah Thomas, 1789), 20. John Pickering, "Introduc-

tion" to *A Vocabulary . . . Peculiar to the United States* (Boston: Hilliard and Metcalf, 1816), 9–10. The remark by Hugh Swinton Legaré and J. W. Simmons is from an editorial in the *Southern Literary Gazette* 1 (1829), quoted in Spencer, 130. Henry Wheaton's statement is from *An Address Pronounced at the Opening of the New-York Athenaeum, December 14, 1824*, 2d ed. (New York: J. W. Palmer, 1825), quoted in Jones, 53.

5. Neal, Everett, Prescott, and Howells quoted in Spencer, *The Quest for Nationality*, 211; Halleck, on 300. T. Watts, "The Future of American Literature," *Eclectic Magazine* 54 (1891): 94; Brander Matthews, "An American Critic on American Literature," *Forum* 43 (1910): 81.

6. See, for example, "On American Literature," *The Dial* 58 (1915): 37–38.

7. For an approving account of this development, see R. E. Spiller, "The Critical Rediscovery of America," in his *Time of Harvest* (New York: Hill & Wang, 1962), 1–8.

8. Richard Ruland reviews the events leading to the establishment of American literature as an academic institution in "The Mission of an American Literary History," *The American Identity*, ed. Rob Kroes (Amsterdam: American Institute of the Univ. of Amsterdam, 1980), 46–64.

9. R. E. Spiller attributes the demise of the idea that American literature is a minor branch of British literature to the work of the social, intellectual, and economic historians, in "The Task of the Historian of American Literature," *Sewanee Review* 43 (1935): 70–79; repr. in his *The Third Dimension* (New York: Macmillan, 1946; repr. 1965), 15–25.

10. Following the pattern set by the teaching of English literature in England, courses in American literature were offered initially in the workingmen's and mechanics' institutes and libraries that sprang up in the northern and midwestern states during the 1820s and 1830s and then in the land-grant universities created for the education of the American working class. Like Oxford and Cambridge, the old patrician colleges of the eastern seaboard were among the very last institutions to offer instruction in the literature of their own country. See Lionel Gossman, "Literature and Education," *New Literary History* 13 (1982): 353.

11. Richard Ruland notes that the founders of the American Literature Section of the Modern Language Association found the ideas of the new social historians so much more consonant with their own than those of the literary fraternity that they seriously considered removing their own shop to the American Historical Association ("The Mission of an American Literary History," 59).

12. These nonlinguistic bases for a definition of American literature are enumerated and evaluated in Benjamin T. Spencer's "An American Literature Again," *Sewanee Review* 57 (1949): 56–72.

13. V. L. Parrington, *Main Currents in American Thought*, 3 vols. (New York: Harcourt Brace, 1927–30). Lionel Trilling, "Reality in America," in *The Liberal Imagination* (New York: Anchor, 1950), 15–32, esp. 20–21. In

1845, Edward W. Johnston doubted that the advocates of a national literature had "any idea of what 'a literature' is"—"American Letters," *The American Review* 1 (1845): 576. A century later, René Wellek concluded from his reading of *The Literary History of the United States* that its editors had no clear conception of either "literature" or "history"—"The Impasse of Literary History," *Kenyon Review* 11 (1949): 500–506.

14. To cite only two examples: Howard Mumford Jones says flatly, "No oral tradition preceded Captain John Smith" (*Theory of American Literature,* 20); and in *The Development of American Romance* (Chicago: Univ. of Chicago Press, 1980), Michael Davitt Bell says that England's "long and distinguished heritage of nonutilitarian literature" was "notably lacking in the colonies" (11).

15. It is worth noticing that *The Literary History of the United States: Bibliography,* ed. R. E. Spiller et al. 3d ed. rev. (New York: Macmillan, 1963) lists studies of British-American literary relations in a section labeled "Mingling of Tongues: Writing Other Than English" (285).

16. The relevance of these three issues to the study of American history is fully stated in Michael Kraus, *The Atlantic Civilization: Eighteenth Century Origins* (Ithaca, N.Y.: Cornell Univ. Press, 1949); Herbert Bolton, *The Spanish Borderlands* (New Haven, Conn.: Yale Univ. Press, 1921); and Max Savelle and Darold D. Wax, *A History of Colonial America,* 3d ed. (Hinsdale, Ill.: Dryden, 1973), respectively.

17. Recent Renaissance studies include *First Images of America,* ed. Fredi Chiapelli et al. 2 vols. (Berkeley, Calif.: Univ. of California Press, 1976); and Stephen Greenblatt, *Renaissance Self-Fashioning: From More to Shakespeare* (Chicago: Univ. of Chicago Press, 1980). J. A. Leo Lemay chides the critics of eighteenth-century British literature for their inattention to contemporaneous American writings, in "Franklin and the *Autobiography:* An Essay on Recent Scholarship," *Eighteenth-Century Studies* 1 (1967/68): 185–211. Exceptions to the rule would have to include Percy Adams, *Travelers and Travel Liars, 1600–1800* (Berkeley, Calif.: Univ. of California Press, 1962). Two nineteenth-century studies that include both British and American writers for purposes other than invidious comparison are Edwin M. Eigner, *The Metaphysical Novel in England and America* (Berkeley, Calif.: The Univ. of California Press, 1978) and Jonathan Arac, *Commissioned Spirits* (New Brunswick, N.J.: Rutgers Univ. Press, 1979).

18. Among the many studies that attempt to connect the British Romantics to the Modernists without assistance from the Americans, some of the more notable are Graham Hough, *The Last Romantics* (London: Duckworth, 1949); Robert Langbaum, *The Poetry of Experience* (New York: Random House, 1957); Frank Kermode, *Romantic Image* (London: Routledge & Kegan Paul, 1957); John Bayley, *The Romantic Survival* (London: Constable, 1957); and David Perkins, *The Quest for Permanence* (Cambridge, Mass.: Harvard Univ. Press, 1959).

19. Quoted in Clarence Gohdes, *American Literature in Nineteenth-*

Century England (Carbondale, Ill.: Univ. of Southern Illinois Press, 1944), 61.

20. On the popularity of the voyage narratives, see L. B. Wright, *Middle-Class Culture in Elizabethan England* (Chapel Hill, N.C.: Univ. of North Carolina Press, 1935), and *The Elizabethans' America* (Cambridge, Mass.: Harvard Univ. Press, 1965); F. T. McCann, *The English Discovery of America to 1585* (New York: King's Crown Press, Columbia Univ., 1952); G. B. Parks, *Richard Hakluyt and the English Voyagers* (New York: American Geographical Society, 1952); D. B. Quinn, *England and the Discovery of America, 1481–1620* (New York: Knopf, 1974); and John Parker, *Books to Build an Empire* (Amsterdam: N. Israel, 1966). On the influence of these writings on sixteenth-century literature, see A. L. Rowse, *The Elizabethans and America* (New York: Harper, 1959); R. R. Cawley, *The Voyagers and Elizabethan Drama* (London: Oxford Univ. Press, 1938), and *Unpathed Waters: Studies in the Influence of the Voyagers on Elizabethan Literature* (Princeton, N.J.: Princeton Univ. Press, 1940); A. B. Giamatti, *The Earthly Paradise and the Renaissance Epic* (Princeton, N.J.: Princeton Univ. Press, 1966); and Harry Levin, *The Myth of the Golden Age in the Renaissance* (Bloomington, Ind.: Indiana Univ. Press, 1969).

21. On the British interest in America during the seventeenth century, see R. W. Frantz, *The English Traveller and the Movement of Ideas, 1600–1732* (Lincoln, Neb.: Univ. of Nebraska Press, 1934); R. R. Cawley, *Milton and the Literature of Travel* (Princeton, N.J.: Princeton Univ. Press, 1951); and Gustav Blanke, *Amerika im englischen Schrifttum des 16. und 17. Jahrhunderts* (Bochum-Langendreer, FRG: Pöppinghaus, 1962).

22. British interest in America during the eighteenth century is dealt with in R. B. Heilman, *America in English Fiction, 1760–1800* (Baton Rouge, La.: LSU Press, 1937); H. N. Fairchild, *The Noble Savage* (New York: Columbia Univ. Press, 1938); Percy Adams, *Travelers and Travel Liars;* B. Bissell, *The American Indian in English Literature of the Eighteenth Century* (New Haven, Conn.: Yale Univ. Press, 1925); and Michael Kraus, *The Atlantic Civilization,* and "Literary Relations Between Europe and America in the Eighteenth Century," *William and Mary Quarterly,* 3d ser., no. 1 (1944): 210–34.

23. On the British reception of American writings in the nineteenth century, see especially Clarence Gohdes, *American Literature in Nineteenth-Century England,* from which much of the following information is taken.

24. On American interest in Britain during the colonial period, see Louis B. Wright, *The Cultural Life of the American Colonies* (New York: Harper & Bros., 1957), and "The Renaissance Tradition in America," in *The American Writer and the European Tradition,* ed. Margaret Denny and W. H. Gilman (New York: McGraw-Hill, 1950; repr. 1964); Michael Kraus, *The North Atlantic Civilization* (Princeton, N.J.: D. Van Nostrand, 1957); R. B. Davis, *Intellectual Life in the Colonial South, 1585–1673,* 3 vols.

(Knoxville, Tenn.: Univ. of Tennessee Press, 1978); E. C. Cook, *Literary Influences in Colonial Newspapers, 1704–1750* (New York: Columbia Univ. Press, 1912); C. A. Herrick, "The Early New Englanders: What Did They Read?" *The Library* 3d ser., 9 (1918): 1–17; C. K. Shipton, "Literary Leaven in Provincial New England," *New England Quarterly* 9 (1936): 203–17; R. M. Myers, "The Old Dominion Looks to London: A Study of English Literary Influences upon the *Virginia Gazette, 1736–1766*," *Virginia Magazine of History and Biography* 54 (1946): 195–217; Robert B. Mowat, *Americans in England* (Boston: Houghton Mifflin, 1935; repr. Freeport, N.Y.: Books for Libraries, 1969); and William L. Sachse, *The Colonial American in Great Britain* (Madison, Wis.: Univ. of Wisconsin Press, 1956).

25. Richard Rush, *A Residence at the Court of London* (London: R. Bentley, 1833), 11–12. On the American interest in British literary culture in the nineteenth century, see William Charvat, *The Origins of American Critical Thought, 1810–1835* (Philadelphia: Univ. of Pennsylvania Press, 1936); Agnes Sibley, *Alexander Pope's Prestige in America* (New York: King's Crown Press, Columbia Univ., 1949); Leon Howard, "The American Revolt Against Pope," *Studies in Philology* 49 (1952): 48–65; W. E. Leonard, *Byron and Byronism in America* (New York: Columbia Univ. Press, 1907); Leon Howard, "Wordsworth in America," *Modern Language Notes* 48 (1933): 359–65; R. E. Spiller, *The American in England During the First Half Century of Independence* (New York: Henry Holt, 1926); Cushing Strout, *The American Image of the Old World* (New York: Harper & Row, 1963); and Philip Rahv, *Britain Through American Eyes* (New York: McGraw-Hill, 1974).

26. On literary relations between England and America, see G. S. Gordon, *Anglo-American Literary Relations* (London: Oxford Univ. Press, 1942); Michael Kraus, *The Atlantic Civilization*, ch. 4, and "Literary Relations Between Europe and America in the Eighteenth Century,"; H. V. Routh, *Towards the Twentieth Century: Essays in the Spiritual History of the Nineteenth* (New York: Macmillan, 1937); H. C. Allen, *The Anglo-American Relationship Since 1783* (London: Adams & Charles Black, 1959); Stephen Spender, *Love-Hate Relations* (New York: Random House, 1974); and Benjamin Lease, *Anglo-American Encounters: England and the Rise of American Literature* (Cambridge: Cambridge Univ. Press, 1982).

27. See Linden Peach, *British Influence on the Birth of American Literature* (New York: St. Martin's Press, 1982).

28. On the problems of defining American English, see Albert H. Marckwardt, *American English* (New York: Oxford Univ. Press, 1958); Albert C. Baugh and Thomas Cable, *A History of the English Language*, 3d ed. (Englewood Cliffs, N.J.: Prentice-Hall, 1978), ch. 11; and C. Merton Babcock, ed., *The Ordeal of American English* (Boston: Houghton Mifflin, 1961).

29. On the relationship between the discovery of America and the in-

vention of printing, see Margaret B. Stillwell, *Incunabula and Americana, 1450–1800* (New York: Cooper Square, 1931), 61–77. Regarding America's impact on the development of modern English, see Wright, *Middle-Class Culture,* 510, 548; Baugh and Cable, *History,* 290–91, 343; and Marckwardt, *American English,* 171.

30. Thomas Pownall, *Memorial Addressed to the Sovereigns of Europe and the Atlantic* (London: J. Debrett, 1803), 9. On the impact of America upon British culture, see F. T. McCann, *The English Discovery of America to 1585;* James E. Gillespie, *The Influence of Oversea Expansion on England to 1700* (New York: Columbia Univ. Press, 1920); J. B. Botsford, *English Society in the Eighteenth Century as Influenced from Oversea* (New York: Macmillan, 1924); G. D. Lillibridge, *Beacon of Freedom: The Impact of American Democracy upon Great Britain, 1830–1870* (Philadelphia: Pennsylvania Univ. Press, 1954); and W. P. Webb, *The Great Frontier* (Austin, Tex.: Univ. of Texas Press, 1964).

31. The passage from *Blackwood's* is quoted in Kraus, *The North Atlantic Civilization,* 70. W. Archer, "America and the English Language," *The Living Age* 219 (1898): 514–19. V. Woolf, "American Fiction," *Saturday Review of Literature* 2 (1 Aug. 1925): 5.

32. L. B. Wright, *Middle-Class Culture,* 510, 548.

33. Stephen Greenblatt, 222–29. R. R. Bolgar discusses the impact of writings about the American aborigines on the reputation of Homer in the European Enlightenment, in "The Greek Legacy," *The Legacy of Greece: A New Appraisal,* ed. M. I. Finley (New York: Oxford, 1982), 462–63.

34. Raymond Williams, *Culture and Society* (New York: Columbia Univ. Press, 1960), esp. ch. 2; his *The Long Revolution* (London: Chatto & Windus, 1961), esp. ch. 7; and William Charvat, "The People's Patronage," in *Literary History of the United States,* 513–25.

35. James Fenimore Cooper, *Notions of the Americans: Picked up by a Travelling Bachelor,* 2 vols. (Philadelphia: Carey, Lea & Carey, 1828) 1:100.

36. See, for example, George Toles, "Charting the Hidden Landscape: *Edgar Huntly*"; and Cynthia Jordan, "On Rereading *Wieland:* The Folly of Precipitate Conclusions"—both in *Early American Literature* 16 (1981): 133–74.

37. Richard P. Adams, "Permutations of American Romanticism," *Studies in Romanticism,* 9 (1970): 249–68; Roger B. Salomon, "Mark Twain and Victorian Nostalgia," in *Patterns of Commitment in American Literature,* ed. Marston La France (Toronto: Univ. of Toronto Press, 1967), 73–91; and John A. Lester, Jr., *Journey Through Despair, 1880–1914: Transformations in British Literary Culture* (Princeton, N.J.: Princeton Univ. Press, 1968), 29.

38. The first of these two views is expressed perfectly by William Charvat—"The shrinkage [in the space given to poets like Bryant, Longfellow, and Whittier in successive histories of American literature] may be

justified on critical but hardly on historical grounds, for the importance of these poets in their own century cannot decrease. We err, as historians, in allowing the taste of the modern reader to nullify the taste of the nineteenth-century reader"—in his essay "Literary Economics," *English Institute Annual, 1949,* ed. Alan S. Downer (New York: Columbia Univ. Press, 1950), 82–83. Van Wyck Brooks formulates the critical view: "The [contemporary] American writer . . . not only has the most meager of birthrights but is cheated out of that. . . . The present is a void, and the American writer floats in that void because the past that survives in the common mind of the present is a past without living value. But is this the only possible past? If we need another past so badly, is it inconceivable that we might discover one, that we might even invent one?" "On Creating a Usable Past," *The Dial* 64 (1918): 338, 339.

39. See, for example, Martin Green, *Re-Appraisals: Some Commonsense Readings in American Literature* (New York: Norton, 1965).

American Things/Literary Things (pp. 143–165)

1. René Wellek, "The Impasse of Literary History," *Kenyon Review* 11 (1949): 500–506. For a frontal assault upon the very idea of American literary history, see Michael Colacurcio, "Does American Literature Have a History?" *Early American Literature* 13 (1978): 110–31. For a critique of the theory and practice of American literary history, especially in the *Literature History of the United States,* see Franz H. Link, *Amerikanische Literaturgeschichtesschreibung, Ein Forschungsbericht* (Stuttgart: Metzler, 1963).

2. Howard Mumford Jones, *The Theory of American Literature,* rev. ed. (Ithaca, N.Y.: Cornell Univ. Press, 1965), 8.

3. René Wellek, "Literary History," in *Literary Scholarship: Its Aims and Methods,* ed. Norman Foerster (Chapel Hill, N.C.: Univ. of North Carolina Press, 1941), 91, 115.

4. Guillén's remark is quoted in Geoffrey Hartmann, "Toward Literary History," *Daedalus* 99 (1970): 380, n. 3. Earl Miner, "Problems and Possibilities of Literary History Today," *Clio* 2 (1973): 219–38. By 1973, Wellek had abandoned all hope for significant progress in the development of a defensible model of literary history. See "The Fall of Literary History," in his *The Attack on Literature and Other Essays* (Chapel Hill, N.C.: Univ. of North Carolina Press, 1982), 64–77.

5. Wellek, "Literary History," 128.

6. Jones, *Theory of American Literature,* 183.

7. D. W. Robertson, "Some Observations on Method in Literary Studies," *New Literary History* 1 (1969): 33.

8. F. L. Pattee, "A Call for a Literary Historian," in *The Reinterpretation of American Literature,* ed. Norman Foerster (New York: Harcourt Brace, 1928), 11.

9. N. Foerster, "Introduction" to *The Reinterpretation of American Literature*, xii.

10. H. H. Clark, "American Literary History and American Literature," in *The Reinterpretation of American Literature*, 190.

11. L. B. Wright, "Toward a New History of American Literature," *American Literature* 12 (1940–41): 283.

12. N. Foerster, "The Literary Historians," *Bookman* 71 (1930): 365.

13. Wellek, "Literary History," 109.

14. A. Schlesinger, Sr., "American History and American Literary History," in *The Reinterpretation of American Literature*, 163–64.

15. Wright, 284.

16. Schlesinger, 162.

17. Pattee, 17.

18. Miner, 230.

19. T. Todorov, "Literary History," in *The Encyclopedic Dictionary of the Sciences of Language*, by T. Todorov and Oswald Ducrot (Baltimore and London: Johns Hopkins Univ. Press, 1972), 144–48. See also Lawrence Stone, "The Revival of Narrative: Reflections on a New Old History," in *The Past and the Present* (Boston, London, and Henley: Routledge & Kegan Paul, 1981), 74–96.

20. Clark, 193; H. S. Canby, "Teaching Our Literature," *Saturday Review of Literature* 3 (1926–27): 493, 499.

21. Clark, 197–98.

22. Lionel Trilling, "Reality in America," in *The Liberal Imagination* (Garden City, N.Y.: Doubleday Anchor Books, 1953), 20–21. For an earlier plea for selecting texts on the basis of literariness rather than Americanness, see Clarence Gohdes, "The Study of American Literature in the United States," *English Studies* 20 (1938): 61–66.

23. Wright, 284. Wright has in mind such historical derivations as that of Yvor Winters, outlined in his accompanying essay, "On the Possibility of a Cooperative History of American Literature," *American Literature* 12 (1940–41): 297–305.

24. William Charvat, "Literary Economics," in *English Institute Annual, 1949*, ed. Alan S. Downer (New York: Columbia Univ. Press, 1950), 82–83.

25. Jones, 145.

26. Richard Chase, *The American Novel and Its Tradition* (Garden City, N.Y.: Doubleday Anchor Books, 1957). Chase's immediate progenitors are F. R. Leavis, *The Great Tradition* (London: George W. Stewart, 1948); and Cleanth Brooks, *Modern Poetry and the Tradition* (Chapel Hill, N.C.: Univ. of North Carolina Press, 1939).

27. Foerster, *The Reinterpretation of American Literature*, xiv. Harry Hayden Clark advises dividing literature itself, along De Quincey's line, into historical and literary subcategories called the literature of "knowledge" and of "power." For still other strategies of the mediatory sort, see

Roy Harvey Pearce, "Historicism Once More" and "Literature, History, Humanism," in *Historicism Once More* (Princeton, N.J.: Princeton Univ. Press, 1969) 3–63; and Leo Marx, "American Studies—a Defense of an Unscientific Method," *New Literary History* 1 (1969): 89. The approaches I call historical and critical Wesley Morris calls "historical relativism" and "subjectivism," in *Toward a New Historicism* (Princeton, N.J.: Princeton Univ. Press, 1972). After outlining the theoretical premises and implications of these conflicting approaches, he surveys the beginnings of a synthetic approach, which he calls "organicist aestheticism," in the work of several critics, especially Murray Krieger.

28. Leo Marx, "Comment [on 'The Aging of America,' by C. Vann Woodward]," *American Historical Review* 82 (1977): 597.

29. Warner Berthoff, "Ambitious Scheme," *Commentary* 44 (1967): 110–114.

30. Claudio Guillén, *Literature as a System: Essays Toward a Theory of Literary History* (Princeton, N.J.: Princeton Univ. Press, 1971), 5–6. See also, René Wellek, *The Rise of English Literary History* (Chapel Hill, N.C.: Univ. of North Carolina Press, 1941).

31. For an instance of this debate, see John Pickering, *A Vocabulary . . . Peculiar to the United States* (Boston: Hilliard & Metcalf, 1816), 9–10, and the editorial by Hugh Swinton Legaré and H. W. Simmons for the *Southern Literary Gazette* 1 (1829), excerpted in Benjamin T. Spencer, *The Quest for Nationality* (Syracuse, N.Y.: Univ. Press, 1957), 130.

32. E. H. Johnson, "American Letters," *The American Review* (June 1845), quoted in Jay B. Hubbell, *Who Are the Major American Writers?* (Durham, N.C.: Duke Univ. Press, 1972), 14. The remaining comments in this paragraph are paraphrased or quoted from *The Native Muse: Theories of American Literature from Bradford to Whitman*, ed. Richard Ruland (New York: E. P. Dutton, 1976), as follows: E. T. Channing (89), Grenville Mellen (209), Longfellow (252), Bryant (147), Cooper (235), and Brownson (398).

33. W. B. Otis, *American Verse, 1625–1807: A History* (New York: Moffatt, Yard, 1909), vii; Henry A. Beers, *An Outline Sketch of American Literature* (New York: Chautauqua Press, 1887), 4; E. C. Stedman, *The Poets of America* (Boston and New York: Houghton Mifflin, 1885), 11; E. C. Stedman and Ellen Hutchinson, eds., *The Library of American Literature,* 11 vols. (New York: C. L. Webster, 1888–90), 1: v.

34. For records of the widening gulf between historical scholarship and literary criticism in the 1940s and 1950s, see Cleanth Brooks, "Literary History vs. Criticism," *Kenyon Review* 2 (1940): 403–12; and W. K. Wimsatt, "History and Criticism: A Problematic Relationship," in his *The Verbal Icon: Studies in the Meaning of Poetry* (Lexington, Ky.: Univ. of Kentucky Press, 1954), 253–65. For a retrospective survey of the movement, see Robert Weimann, "Past Significance and Present Meaning in Literary History," *New Literary History,* (1969): 91–109. And for a review

of the whole development of American literary historiography in this century, see Richard Ruland, "The Mission of American Literary History," in *The American Identity,* ed. Rob Kroes (Amsterdam: American Institute, Univ. of Amsterdam, 1980), 46–64.

35. Hubbell, 261.

36. Louis J. Budd, E. H. Cady, and C. L. Anderson, eds., *Toward a New American Literary History* (Durham, N.C.: Duke Univ. Press, 1980).

37. Wellek, "Literary History," 129.

38. Questions regarding the relations between "literature" and "history" can take various forms having to do with the impact of extraliterary forces upon writing, the use of literary texts as historical sources, and the literariness of historiography. While these are perfectly legitimate questions, they are not my concern in this essay, which deals exclusively with the problem of writing a history of literature. For discussions of these other issues, see Rosalie Colie, "Literature and History," in *Relations of Literary Study,* ed. James Thorpe (New York: Modern Language Association of America, 1967), 1–26; Robert H. Bremmer, ed., *Essays on History and Literature* (Columbus, Ohio: Ohio State Univ. Press, 1966); and R. H. Canary and H. Kozicki, eds., *The Writing of History* (Madison, Wis.: Univ. of Wisconsin Press, 1978).

39. See, for example, Wellek, "Literary History," 106; and Claudio Guillén, *Literature as a System.*

40. See. for example Wellek, "Literary History," 124, 125; and F. W. Bateson, *English Poetry and the English Language,* 2d ed. (New York: Russell and Russell, 1961), 6. Robertson, 22.

41. See, for example, Wellek, "Literary History," 107.

42. On the limitations of *Stoffegeschichte,* see René Wellek and Austin Warren, *Theory of Literature* (New York: Harcourt Brace, 1956), 250; and Michael Riffaterre, "The Stylistic Approach to Literary History," in *New Directions in Literary History,* ed. Ralph Cohen (London: Routledge & Kegan Paul, 1974), 160, n.23.

43. For a critical review of *Rezeptionästhetik,* see Robert C. Holub, *Reception Theory* (New York: Methuen, 1984). For an application of this theory to American literary history, see Steven J. Mailloux, *Interpretive Conventions: The Reader in the Study of American Fiction* (Ithaca, N.Y.: Cornell Univ. Press, 1982), 159–91.

44. Roger Fowler, *The Language of Literature* (London: Routledge & Kegan Paul, 1971), 88–91.

45. This is not to say that languages exist ideally, independent of their use, only that they exist independent of their use in any selection of texts. See Robertson, 26.

46. For a somewhat more elaborate rendition of this idea, see Seymour Katz, "'Culture' and Literature in American Studies," *American Quarterly* 20 (1968): 328–29.

47. The theory offered here is to be distinguished from those of F. W.

Bateson, in *English Poetry and the English Language,* and Josephine Miles, in four books: *The Vocabulary of Poetry* (Berkeley and Los Angeles: Univ. of California Press, 1946), *The Continuity of Poetic Language* (1951), *Renaissance, Eighteenth-Century, and Modern Language in English Poetry: A Tabular View* (1960), and *Eras and Modes in English Poetry,* rev. ed. (Westport, Conn.: Greenwood Press, 1964). Neither Bateson nor Miles defines literature historically, as writing that contributes significantly to the development of language. As a result, both must fall back on supposedly timeless aesthetic standards for the identification of literary texts, which they then treat, necessarily, as passive reflections of linguistic change caused by external forces. This omission leads Wellek to regard Bateson's theory as one more case of a literary history dependent upon extraliterary history ("Literary History," 107).

48. Wellek, "Literary History," 107.

49. Miner, 229.

50. Michael Riffaterre, in "The Stylistic Approach to Literary History," 147–64, for example, places certain poetic words, phrases, and sentences in the context of "linguistic codes" that appear and disappear over time in French and offers these identifiable codes in place of such protean concepts as "poetic language," "Romanticism," and "literature," which provide the customary bases for idealist and comparatist literary histories.

51. James Fenimore Cooper, *Notions of the Americans . . .,* 2 vols. (Philadelphia: Carey, Lea, and Carey, 1828), 1: 100.

52. This is another point at which Bateson and Miles go astray. Although both set out to rescue English literary history from the nationalists by grounding it in linguistic change, both obscure that historical ground by dividing it into political subsectors. In his preface to the 1961 edition of *English Poetry and the English Language,* Bateson congratulates British English and British poetry for having repulsed the "foreign" invasions led by Eliot and Yeats (6); and in *Eras and Modes in English Poetry,* Miles attempts to isolate an "American mode" stemming from British poetry of the seventeenth century and developing along a totally independent line thereafter (224–48). This notion that the British settlement of North America divided the language into two separate streams, added to their earlier failure to grasp the functional role of poetry in the development of language, prevents Bateson and Miles from seeing how modern English has in fact evolved and thus from erecting a coherent literary history upon that evolutionary framework.

53. Fowler, 93; Robertson, 28; Katz, 328–29.

54. America's influence on the development of modern English is reviewed in Randolph Quirk, *The English Language and Images of Matter* (London: Oxford Univ. Press, 1972), chs. 1–2.

55. Regarding the reformation of the American literary canon in the light of modernism, see Malcolm Cowley, *Exile's Return,* rev. ed. (New York: Viking, 1956), 296–300; Richard Ruland, *The Rediscovery of Ameri-*

can Literature (Cambridge, Mass.: Harvard Univ. Press, 1967); and Jay B. Hubbell, *Who Are the Major American Writers?*, 155–200.

56. In "Literary Theory, Criticism, and History," René Wellek argues that these three activities can be integrated only upon an absolute common ground. In "The Concept of Evolution in Literary History," however, he dismisses the implicitly absolutist models of literary evolution employed by the Aristotelian organicists, Hegelian dialecticians, and New Critical formalists and proposes in their stead a more relativistic model that acknowledges the role played by readers, as well as writers, in the constitution of literary texts and their historical relations. This latter essay also identifies Bateson and Miles as the only practicing evolutionists among Western literary historians and thus identifies at least three of the factors that my historical model attempts to incorporate: linguistic evolution, the role of literature in that evolution, and the dependence of that evolutionary structure upon the historical point from which it is viewed. Wellek's two essays appear in *Concepts of Criticism,* ed. Stephen G. Nichols, Jr. (New Haven, Conn.: Yale Univ. Press, 1963), 1–20, 37–53.

57. Ruland, *Rediscovery,* 281.